How to Get from Passion to Success: The Hypnotic Journey

RICHARD BARKER

All rights reserved. No portion of this book may be reproduced, stored in a retrieval system, or transmitted in any form or by any means—electronic, mechanical, photocopy, recording, scanning, or other,—except for brief quotations in critical reviews or articles, without the prior written permission of the publisher.

CopyRight Richard Barker 2018

DEDICATION

I dedicate this book to all those who are striving for self-improvement. To those willing to go the extra mile and those willing to create a better version of themselves. I dedicate this book to the lifelong learners and to those who dare to dream about their future.

I dedicate this book to my online self-help group called Richards Angels. This group of individuals have created a group that care and accept you, no matter who you are. They understand and run on the assumption of arriving at their purpose through their pain. This group help and supports those less fortunate or who are going through health issues and trauma. Through the power of encouragement and support #richardsangels lift each other up and support and nurture one another. Incredible Hypnotist Richards Angels can be joined on Facebook

I dedicate this book to Silvia, for taking the fight against cancer head on and winning, for inspiring many around you to tackle and deal with illness and for showing me immense love and support. I dedicate this book to all of the angels that walk the planet earth. It is truly for you that I write these words. I am humbled by the love and support that has been shown to be during some of my challenging moments.

INTRODUCTION

"Do you find yourself unable to stick to your plans or goals"

"Do you need help overcoming habits you have formed that do not help you get closer to your dream life"

" Are you clueless about how to start focusing on your own self-discovery and mindfulness"

"Do you find yourself just stuck in the mud without direction"

You have something special inside you. Something you know. Something you do. Something you can teach. You feel like you should be doing more. We all have this something special inside of us and, if we use it right, we can change our habits, our outcomes and our world.

You will gain valuable information within the pages of this book which will equip you with powerful tools to help you shape your life and journey. Your new way of thinking and motivation will ultimately attract interest, increase desire, demand attention, and promote a better you. You will become successful and unstoppable at whatever it is you set out to achieve. Information alone isn't enough. It's the skillful application of the right information at the right time that can change your life. You will be guided through the process of the Hypnotic Journey and How To Get From Passion To Success.

Where are you now with your life? Discouraged you don't have direction? Your goals will take too long? You are working too hard and stuck in a rut? You don't earn enough money? all that is about to change

In this book

"You will learn how to master your own thoughts and reach mindfulness"
"Discover way in which you can reach and exceed your goals"
"Master the essential techniques to self-hypnosis and gaining guided focus"

My name is Richard Barker and I have been studying human behavior for 3 decades. In the last 10 years though, it has become more apparent to me that people consistently seem to fail at not only goal setting and the targets of those goals, but also keeping resolutions and promises to themselves. As a hypnotist I understand the power of your Neurotransmitters and the manifestation of thought processes and how they can turn into actions. Sticking to your goals and keeping on track is vital to your future success habits and dreams that you aspire to fulfill.
Many successful people will tell you several things

1. What gets measured gets done. If you measure and focus on your goals, they will become a reality

2. Holding yourself accountable brings you closer to your goals

3. Simply the action of writing things down brings you more in alignment with your wants and needs

4. Documenting the journey to success is more important than arriving

5. By being consistent and persistent you will get to where you want to be

With your passion, intention, attention, and patience, you will achieve and attain the life you set out to achieve. You'll get respect for being that goal setter, habit changer and motivator and achiever, your business and social life will flourish, you'll make lifetime income, and you'll love the adventure. So turn the page and begin now!

Sincerely,

Richard Barker
Incredible Hypnotist

CONTENTS

	Introduction	IV
	Acknowledgments	VIII
1	Getting that passion	1
2	Self discovery	33
3	Take control of your mind	77
4	Get and stay motivated	94
5	Get into mindfulness	117
6	Increase your focus	132
7	Getting a smarter brain	145
8	Unstoppable confidence	170
9	Avoiding red mist	197
10	Direction and determination	217
11	Hypnotic success habits	228
12	Hypnotic goals	259
13	Self hypnosis	283
14	Growing as an entrepreneur	304

1 GETTING THAT PASSION

Do you ever feel as though you are just going through the motions? Do you ever feel as though you're drifting through life without ever really getting any sense of inspiration, engagement, or excitement?

Does life sometimes feel like a series of uninteresting chores?

Or perhaps you're perfectly happy and comfortable but you rarely feel challenged or excited. Maybe you spend most of your evenings on the sofa watching TV. Or even out at the pub with friends. Maybe you spend your whole life picking up after your children. Have you developed some habits you wish to get rid of? Are you generally deflated or not sure on your direction in life?

Look at people like Albert Einstein, Newton, Picasso, Mozart, Winston Churchill, Neil Armstrong, Nelson Mandela, Mother Teresa, among others.

Now look at your own life. Is there a bit of a stark difference?

And are you *really* happy the way you are currently feeling? Or do you feel on some level as though there are better uses of your time? could you be the next legend? are you a secret Rock Star or motivational speaker waiting to burst onto the scene?

Whether you're happy or you feel in a funk, the truth is that life gets a *whole* lot better as soon as you fill it with *meaning*.

That means finding your life's purpose. Finding the thing that you're passionate about and then focussing on that. I was in the British Army for 7 years and a Police Officer for 10 years but didn't find my true meaning until I became a Hypnotist. It took time to navigate the path and truly find my purpose on earth, but I found it.

As soon as you find meaning you will unlock entirely different levels of focus, of inspiration, of engagement, of charisma. Life suddenly has structure, it makes sense, and you become far more alive. You stop daydreaming and sleepwalking through life and you instead begin to forge your own meaningful path.

You will get more out of the time you have on this earth, and truly there is little that is more worthwhile than that.

When you find your purpose, you'll even become healthier... even become *more attractive*.

It won't matter whether success follows because you'll be contented with spending your days pursuing this thing *without* any kind of financial reward.

But success very likely *will* come. Read on and discover why that is and why finding your purpose is what you need in order to change *everything*. People like you want to be more successful in their life, but actually knowing how to take the steps needed to achieve that success can be mystifying. Even when you understand what is required, it can be extremely challenging to take action unless you know where you are going. Most people stumble blindly along, not understanding why they continue to fail at their efforts. But this book is going to change all of that for you. I am going to connect your success habits hypnotically so that you refuse to fail. This journey is about discovery and progress, I am excited, are you?

So, why is it that finding your purpose can change everything? How does this help you to truly come alive? Why is this the *key* to success?

Have you ever heard someone tell you that they find passion to be a turn on? *Many* women say that they love seeing men who speak passionately about a subject. Why do you think that rock stars get so many groupies? It's not just about the fame: if you go to a rock concert to see a *relative unknown band*, they will still almost always have the admiration of the opposite and even same sex or gender! The simple fact is that they're doing what they love, they're demonstrating skill and passion on stage and to the adulation of countless others. That's a turn on! Ask yourself something, when your partner or someone you feel attracted to is at their sexiest. Is it when they are talking about something they find absolutely fascinating? Or when they are hard at work programming, or working out at the gym? Think of that sexy violinist all in black, who is taken away by the music and who has the crowd eating out of their hand. Or an incredible dancer.

In fact, finding passion can actually be a trick for bringing more romance and excitement back into your relationship. It is seeing someone who is highly motivated and driven, who is passionate about what they do. When you spend all day on the couch with someone, the magic goes. You become too close. It's hard to *want* what you already have.

We don't just become sexually more attractive when we're focussing on our passion: we become more attractive in the visceral most basic way. Attractive in the sense that people want to be around us, to listen to us, to follow us. We become leaders, inspirers, beacons.

The reason is that we enter what is known as a flow state. A flow state occurs when you are focussed on something 100%. When you are so engaged with whatever you are doing, that all other distractions fall aside. More importantly, the part of your brain associated with your sense of self and with your self *regulation* shuts down. This is the dorsal-lateral prefrontal cortex.

This removes the parts of our brain that usually holds us back and that prevents us from being 100% in the moment. In other words, we are no longer worrying about our finances or about what other people think. Instead, we are highly focussed and 100% of our mental and energy resources are directed toward that event.

And what happens when you direct 100% of your resources toward one activity? Well, it should come as no shock to hear that you become *better* at that one activity!

In sports, flow states can cause time to almost seem to slow down and dilate, giving us more time to react to things that are happening around us. When we're writing an essay or painting a masterpiece, we see increased activity in the medial prefrontal cortex, giving us better focus on what's happening inside our own mind and almost seeming to *shut out* the rest of the world. I work with several athletes in my hypnosis practice and when they play the game or sport using guided self-hypnotic focus, they always achieve higher results.

These are different kinds of flow states but they both represent the same thing: being highly focussed and highly engaged with whatever it is that you're doing and therefore performing your best.

And this is actually a highly exhilarating experience. Many people describe it as almost euphoric and enlightening: they feel so switched on and so alive because they're forgetting all of their worries and all of their concerns for that brief amount of time: it's almost as if they are in a hypnotic state. They love the thing they're doing *so much* that nothing else seems to matter, at least for a time. Hypnosis can quickly and easily put you into this state.

And from a neuro chemical standpoint, this makes sense too: the brain floods itself with not only focus neurotransmitters (similar to hormones) but also endorphins to make us feel good.

And this is also the state you need to be in if you want to be highly successful. Because countless studies show us that great things happen when you're in flow. It has been suggested that the vast majority of world records have been broken by people who were in flow states at the time. And it has also been suggested that all the most successful start-ups are in flow too.

Getting to this point is *all about* being highly engaged with what you're doing and it's all about *loving* that thing.

Because flow is triggered by the salience network. This is the part of the brain (the anterior cingulate cortex and other connected areas) which tells us what's important and what we should be focussed on. It does this via the release of dopamine – the 'reward hormone' – which our brains produce in anticipation of reward.

In other words, dopamine tells us that something is important and that it requires our attention. This directs the salience network – the attention network – toward the relevant brain areas. That in turn ensures that we remain focussed on those things and allows our sense of 'self' to fade away.

Flow states *can* occur when we're in danger. This is why we often enjoy split-second reflexes when we're snowboarding down the side of a mountain at break-neck speed. When this happens our brain comes alive and says 'I REALLY need to pay attention to this'.

But when you LOVE what you do, the same thing happens. When you love what you do, the brain says 'I REALLY need to pay attention'. This time it's because you're so engaged with that task and so enraptured by it, that nothing else seems to share the same importance.

Magnetism and Passion

Others can sense this passion and this focus and it sends powerful signals that you are someone highly capable, highly exciting to be around and highly engaging.

Have you ever noticed how some people seem to be highly charismatic? Have you ever met someone who you just instantly wanted to like you? Someone who just won you over and was highly persuasive and exciting?

These are people we consider to be highly charismatic. And from where does charisma come?

Studies show us that charisma is positively correlated with gesticulation: when someone moves around a lot while they talk, when they make lots of hand gestures as they explain something, when they seem more *animated*. That's when they become charismatic, charming and engaging.

Why? Because we interpret this as someone being 100% behind what they're saying. When they move around and gesticulate, their body language is *congruent* with what they're saying. They appear to really believe it!

And therefore, they become far more engaging and magnetic. We interpret this as: 'Well if *they* seem that excited by what they're saying, maybe I should listen too!'.

This could even be explained by mirror neurons: neurons that fire when we witness someone doing or saying something and the same neurons fire in our own brains as though *we* were doing that thing. When we see someone come alive with passion and enthusiasm, we *literally* feel that passion and enthusiasm ourselves to some degree!

And there's one more BIG reason that life gets so much better when you find your passion or your drive. That is because you'll discover what it is that you're really want to accomplish, you'll have a goal and you'll have an endpoint. And when you have that, you'll know precisely what you need to do. You'll be able to prioritize and you'll be able to shoot for the stars.

The human brain loves challenge, it loves growth and it loves forward momentum. When we feel like we've achieved a goal – even a small one – we release neurotransmitters and hormones that make us feel good. And this helps the brain to change shape and grow and develop.

But conversely, when we spend every day doing the same thing, it leaves us with no incentive for change. And when you don't grow, you remain static. And then you decay. This is literally what happens in the brain: if you don't use your brain to its fullest potential, then it *will* start to atrophy. It becomes less plastic. And the chemical balance makes us more prone to depression and indifference.

Having something we love to do gives us a goal and a purpose. This gives us a trajectory. And this stops every day from feeling the same. It stops every day from being a slog toward… nothing in particular. And simply having that journey makes us so much happier and more fulfilled.

It doesn't even matter if you manage to turn your passion into your career. It doesn't matter if you ever get acknowledgement for it. Simply HAVING that passion and having a goal and a journey… it puts everything else into perspective and it gives life meaning.

Injecting Meaning Into Every Day
So, our goal is to find life's purpose. And hopefully, you've already understood a little bit about why this is such a worthwhile and meaningful endeavor and such a good use of your time.

But this takes a lot of work. You're not going to get there overnight. In the meantime, there's a lot more you need to accomplish.

It starts by injecting more meaning into every day. The aim is not only to find a purpose and a goal to work toward, but also to make those more mundane parts of your life more important, impactful and rewarding.

Because in reality, most of us aren't going to be able to give up our other endeavors. You're unlikely to have the option anytime soon to give up your job and embrace a career doing whatever it is you love full time. You're still going to need to clean the dishes; you'll still want to spend time with friends.

You'll still need to go to the shops to get bread, and you'll need to stick with your day job.

If you find your purpose and then give yourself only a few hours in the week to focus on it, this can actually be even more distressing in some ways.

Once you know what it is that you really want to be doing, how you really want to be spending your time… it can become torturous to find yourself stuck in an office 9-5, or to have to spend your evenings tidying, all the while knowing precisely what you'd rather be doing.

So, you need to find ways to make everything that little bit more meaningful. To start putting color back into your life.

I want you to think back over the past few weeks and months. What is it that you have achieved? What is it that you have done? What are your fondest memories?

Chances are, you're drawing some blanks. The chances are that you don't know what you did because you can't remember.

And that's because what you did had no meaning.

When you go through the same routines every day, when you do the same things... your life doesn't have much meaning or much impact. Why *would* you remember a night where you watched the same show and ate the same thing that you do *every* night? It all blends into one.

And there's actually a logical reason why all this happens.

Remember that dopamine that is released when our brains think we're doing something highly important? Well, that very same chemical is also partly responsible for encouraging the formation of memories. More specifically, an increase in dopamine is correlated with an increase in BDNF – Brain Derived Neurotrophic Factor. This in turn is responsible for increasing our 'brain plasticity', which in short means that our neurons form more connections and we gain new knowledge and memories.

When nothing important or exciting happens, no new connections are formed. When something important happens, *far* more connections are formed.

And the most extreme example of this is the 'Flashbulb Memory'. A flashbulb memory is a phenomenon studied in neuroscience. It occurs when something of seemingly great importance happens and it causes us to form an incredibly vivid and detailed memory.

So, the more meaning you have in your life, the more you will find you remember. If yours is a life where every day is an adventure, where every day brings new excitement, then you will fill your brain with countless detailed memories.

And when you look back over your recent weeks and years they will seem full and nearly endless.

Our perception of time is entirely reliant on our memories. That's why a day can seem longer when you do lots of things.

So, the more you do, the more memories you have, the longer your life will have seemed to be! In that way, by putting life in your years, you LITERALLY put years in your life.

If you spend every day doing the same thing, you'll look back on your life and have no new memories, no excitement. It will all blur into one nothingness and your life will seem to move faster, to be shorter.

So, is it any wonder that a life without meaning leads to depression and that feeling of claustrophobia and funk?

The answer starts with novelty.

To understand this, you need to understand how the brain and its memory systems work. Or more importantly, you need to understand *why* they are there in the first place. What are they for?

The answer is that your brain stores memories that it thinks are going to be useful for your survival and those that it thinks will help you to avoid danger in future, or to pursue valuable goals and valuable achievements.

And the perfect example of this is novelty.

When you go through the same routine every single day, you activate the precise same neural networks. These become more and more deeply ingrained, more and more highly myelinated and insulated. Thus, signals will travel much more quickly and effectively through those neural connections and you will become better at doing that one thing. But there's no need for new neurons and new memories. And you can almost do those things on autopilot!

But when you put yourself in an entirely new environment, or when you challenge yourself with an entirely new task, you need to pay attention. Your current skill set is not equipped to deal with this situation. Thus, your brain needs to pay attention and it needs to *learn* fast.

If you are someone who never exposes themselves to anything new, then this can almost be overwhelming for the brain. You might find yourself feeling intimidated, stressed and scared and not in a good way! This is why some people will seldom *ever* step outside their comfort zones. But you need to go through with it anyway – and repeatedly – if you are to eventually overcome this and make your brain more plastic and adaptable again.

So, in short, you need to subject yourself to new things. You need to subject yourself to new experiences. And you need to be brave and bold.

Then your life will be more challenging, more adventurous, and ultimately *far* more memorable.

There is so much to see and do, to try and to experiment with that you can try right now. Even small things will help make your life richer and more interesting. Now when someone asks you how your day is, you'll actually have something interesting to say in response!

Our brain assigns meaning to adventure and without adventure, we are left feeling a sense of emptiness.

And one more key takeaway here is the movement. Our lack of movement and our being confined to one spot *literally* causes our bodies and our minds to waste away. Get out there. Get exploring. Try new things. Otherwise, you doom yourself to a very slow but very certain demise.

The Science of Awe

Let's take a moment to engage in a little experiment. I want you to stop what you're doing and then picture the most *meaningful* thing you can picture. What is the 'archetypal' meaningful experience? If you had to paint an inspiring and meaningful image, what would you paint?

I can almost guarantee that in thinking about this, your mind will have turned at least momentarily to a sunset, a mountain, or some other kind of vista. These images are powerful and moving and they are what we associated strongly with meaningful experiences and existence.

In fact, there is even a growing practice of 'awe cultivation'. Awe cultivation refers to the practice of seeking out and inciting awe-inspiring moments in order to fill your life with more meaning.

These are moments when our breath is taken away by the scope of a scene, by the scale of natural beauty, or by a living creature so alien and magnificent that we can't handle it.

What is happening during these moments?

Scientists are not entirely sure, but one of the most popular theories is that awe is caused by a huge shift in perception or perspective.

Human beings are inherently egocentric and self-centered. We care only about ourselves and about our own petty concerns.

But when we are faced with a valley that is so magnificent in scope that we feel absolutely microscopic, this forces us to reassess the importance of our own lives. It forces us to recognize our place in the universe.

The same thing happens when we watch a documentary and learn something that completely changes the way we see things.

Of course, this has a similarly positive effect of helping us to let go of our own concerns for a moment – just like being highly engaged with what we're doing. And it has also been explained as being so positive because it helps us to overcome the feeling of not having enough time, because the world seems so vast and impossible.

Spend some time trying to have your mind *blown*.

Here's another way to find out whether or not your life has meaning and to see what the difference between a meaningful life and mundane, uninspiring one is.

And that is to ask yourself this question: would your life make a good book?

If your life were a film, would you watch it?

And would your character be an inspiring hero, or a dullard?

If your life is not interesting enough to make for a good story, then how can it possibly be considered an exciting or interesting one?

And so, we can use this to work backward. What is it that makes these stories so interesting? How can we turn our lives into one of these epic stories?

Well, one way to start out is by looking at the basics of narrative structure. By assessing how an author might go about approaching a story.

And this will often mean using a proven structure that is known as 'The Hero's Journey'.

The hero has been around since storytelling began, and is featured in almost every story and religion from the ancient world to current Sci-Fi blockbusters. Normally, the story begins with the hero being sent on some sort of quest. The background of the hero is normally that they're something of an outsider and maybe have adopted parents or deceased parents (and often this is what triggers their leaving to embark on the journey). This stage is known as 'crossing the threshold' and it is the point at which the rules of their world are turned upside down, or they physically journey to a new land. Think of Neo exiting the Matrix, think of Dorothy landing in Oz, think of Frodo leaving the Shire, or think even of something less obvious – like Shallow Hal gaining his new sight.

In many ways, this is similar to that moment of 'awe' that completely changes our perception.

During this journey they will meet an old mentor near the beginning (/surrogate Father figure) who will train them in some of their abilities. They will also likely be given an important gift by this mentor that will help them on their quest (originally a sword though this varies). They will likely also encounter a side kick who will help them on their journey and meet a 'trickster' who will be neither friend nor foe but act as another foil for our protagonist (though the trickster is often eventually allied to the hero and can be pivotal in taking down the main enemy). Along the journey the hero will also take on several smaller challenges each bringing them closer to their final objective and their nemesis. Once these smaller challenges are completed they will encounter the architect of their troubles – the overbearing nemesis who will likely hold a damsel captive.

This often involves entering a dark and foreboding place, which is often referred to as 'the belly of the beast' or the 'innermost cave'. There, they do battle in what is known as 'the ordeal'.

At this point the hero is often seemingly killed but undergoes a 'rebirth' coming back stronger and more powerful to slay the captor (also often portrayed as a dragon), save the damsel, win the gold and return to their village a hero. This transformation is the apotheosis.

So how do you go about making sure you have your own hero's journey? How do you make your life less about pushing pencils and more about discovering incredible things, going to incredible places, taking on amazing challenges? The answer is to adventure to new places, meet new people and to make sure that you grow. Cross thresholds, change and seek out new treasures – all the things we've discussed so far!

So, discovering new things, trying new things, using your body, challenging yourself… these are all things that will help you to feel alive and to add meaning to your life.

But there is another way to add meaning. And that is to spend more time with others. To do more things with other people.

This is incredibly important. Why? Because spending time with others is another thing that adds meaning to what we do.

What we do now, echoes through eternity…

Look at it this way, if you were to spend all of your time alone at home and never speak to anyone or stop going on Facebook, then you could die and no one would know until the smell disturbed the neighbors. This is a sad thought indeed but it's also, unfortunately, entirely true.

And therefore, *nothing* you do will have any lasting impact. If you were to have the most incredible day – but not report it – you would die having made no change to the world.

This underscores the importance of our interactions with others. If we have no one to share our experiences with, then they can have no real meaning and no impact that extends past our own lives.

Creating lasting works is another way to achieve a similar form of immortality of course, but that's something that you can't guarantee. Not all of us have it in us to create something that will change the world. But we can *all* make friends and do things that will help them to feel happier and that will help them to remember us when we're gone.

So, it comes down to emotion. And our emotions are all based on our subconscious brain and our neuroscience – as well as our evolution.

And from an evolutionary standpoint, there are few things more important than social interaction. Our social interactions keep us safe, they provide us with access to resources and they provide us with the opportunity to learn and to find friends.

And they are also fantastic for our brain. Social interactions trigger the release of endorphins and other hormones. And they help us to form new neural connections. And what is more, is they are one of the key things that help our brains to develop.

There will be times when your purpose is at odds with other people. How about when you are spending all your time painting or spending all your money developing your business plan and your wife or husband misses you or is worried about finances?

This is why one of THE most important things to do is to explain yourself to your partner. To let them know what's important to you, who you are. You owe them your honesty. Hopefully, they'll be on the same page as you. But if they're not? Ask for forgiveness, not permission. If you let someone else clip your wings, then you'll only end up resenting them. Show them the beauty of your passion and enjoy it together.

What's even better for creating meaning in our lives is helping others. When we help others, this actually creates one of the *biggest* neurochemical hits there is. This helps us to feel far more confident in who we are. It helps us to get a sense of having done something worthwhile and of having made a lasting impact on the world. This is called the 'helper's high' and it is actually considered another 'flow trigger'.

And interestingly, awe cultivation has actually been shown to *make us* more likely to be altruistic and giving. It's all coming together!

MANY people say that they get the most satisfaction out of helping others and giving back.

So, if you're looking for that meaning, if you want to feel as though you're contributing something, then consider charity work. That might mean giving some money but better yet is to get out there and help. That could mean spending time with lonely elderly people, it could mean working as a Samaritan and answer phone calls to people who may be considering suicide

Stand For Something

We live in a very shallow age, and although it's no one's fault, it's really a terrible shame that most of us don't stand for anything real or important anymore. Sure, we all have hobbies and interests, and we all probably have goals and beliefs, but how many of us actually use our beliefs to inform our big decisions in life? And how many of us actively try to make a difference in our chosen area of interest so that we can go to bed feeling as though we've touched the lives of others in a real and impactful way?

The fact is that most of us just don't give much thought to what we stand for, or how we can make that stand and have the strength to follow our convictions. And when you don't know what you stand for, it makes it hard to know what's important. This is another reason that we can get very stressed and very upset about something petty – like our number of Instagram likes.

Not only that, but not having any beliefs in this sense actually makes you vulnerable in terms of being more easily led. If you don't know what you stand for, what's to stop someone from convincing you that their way is right?

As Alice Cooper sang: if you don't stand for something, you will fall for anything.

We all stand for lots of things. If you follow British football a lot, for instance, then you might stand for Man United, or the Bills if you prefer the NFL, while at the same time if you're a graphic designer in your day job you could also stand for the importance of 'good design'.

But when someone asks what you stand for overall, you are unlikely to answer with either of these ideas. Rather, we generally tend to assume that the thing we stand for first and foremost will be something more fundamental and that will have wider implications on the world. So how do you decide on that?

One way to decide what to stand for is to look at what's central to all your other beliefs and interests. For me, I love traveling, I love hypnosis and I love coming up with unique and interesting marketing ideas. So, what's the common thread here? It's freedom - it's not being tied down and it's being able to make the most of life as a result. I also find self-improvement very important, and I believe that this is what enables you to gain more freedom.

By looking at the things that are most important to you and that drive the various areas of your life, you should be able to find common threads that give you your 'purpose'. What brings you joy and happiness? What is stopping others from feeling that way?

Likewise, what brings you sadness? When have you been hurt or mistreated? And how can you help others to *avoid* that same fate?

Likewise, ask what gets you riled up. When are you most angry? When you feel that rage bubbling up, go with it. Let it move you. I talk about "Red Mist" later in this book too and how to avoid it.

So, once you've decided what you stand for, how do you go about living that life? Well, of course, you can donate to charities, you can talk to others about your beliefs and spread the word, and you can live your life in accordance with your values which is most important of all. If your job, your passions and the way you conduct your relationships all are in accordance with the things that drive you, then you will be sure to lead a fulfilled life and help others at the same time.

And most importantly, don't let anyone make you compromise on those beliefs and principles. This pride and passion will help to guide you.

Finding Purpose

Finding meaning in everything you do will bring you greater happiness and purpose and will make your life far more fulfilling. You'll be happier and all your petty troubles will seem so much less important.

Not only will you gain that focus and commitment that comes from knowing what you want from life, but you'll also provide yourself with the stimulus, the growth, the purpose and the forward momentum that you need to keep on pushing forward.

Having a goal and a purpose gives you a direction and that helps you to make sense of everything else.

So how do you find it?

Often, the key comes down to what you love to do. We can sometimes struggle even to answer this seemingly simple question though, so here are a few exercises to help you find the answer:

- Ask when the last time you were truly happy was

- Ask when you were *at your happiest*

- If you had to spend a week doing one thing, what would it be?

- If you visualize your perfect future, what does it look like?

- What would you do right now, if you could do anything?

- What did you love doing when you were younger, before you become old and jaded?

These questions can help to start to uncover your true callings and your passions.

At the same time, you should also think about what you are good at and you should think in terms of everything we've discussed so far about meaning.

In other words, what are you really good at? Have you had a lot of success in any area of your life or career? Do you find that certain things come very easily to you? Do you find that you've kind of been swept up by the current?

Now think back to the things that you stand for and that make you feel most passionate. Now think about the people with who you like spending time.

And when was the last time you felt *awe*?

What is a worthy challenge for you?

The question starts to take on a shape. It starts to become: what is it that you have to OFFER?

As the old question goes: don't ask what the world can do for you, ask what you can do for the world. And that, cheesy though it might be, is the key.

Because that is *inherently* going to mean you follow your gifts and your callings, it means you'll inherently be doing things that are difficult and that have lasting impact on others.

You should be motivated by more than just money and more than just entertainment. Let's face it, if we really were only motivated by what we'd like to be doing right now, then we'd all say that 'eating, sleeping and sex' were pretty much our passions (maybe even in that order).

Instead, ask as well:

- What are you not happy with?
- What power do you have to change the world for the better?
- Who can you influence?
- How do you want to be remembered?

Writing your eulogy as you would like to hear it can help you to think about how you want to be remembered. So, what do you want people to say about you after you're gone? Once you've done this you can then think about how you need to live your life in order to ensure that is how you'd be remembered.

But then there's the middle question: the 'why'.

Why do you want to do this? Who is it for? What drives you?

And the best companies answer this. Look at Google, it's not just about selling products – it's about a vision to organize all the world's information.

Apple was at its peak when it focused on doing things differently: on being more personal, more stylish, more simple and more user-centric than the big technology firms like IBM.

Even companies like Red Bull are more successful because they have found a calling – Red Bull is all about performance and sports and amazing world records.

One of the most important tips of all is that you should be *completely* honest with yourself.

In other words, don't say what you *think* you should say. Don't say you want to help other people and give money to charity if you don't really.

Don't say you want to be the ethical lawyer because you love the thrill of the chase if *really* you love anime.

Your calling might not be noble, or honorable, or exciting. It might be lame. It might be highly inconvenient. But all of this only works when you follow your heart and your intuition.

Likewise, don't be trapped by the things you once said. If you change your mind then embrace it – don't keep forcing forward with something once the love has gone. Otherwise, you're just a slave to your superego.

A vision is the end destination. A goal is part of a plan – a milestone on the way to that destination. We talk about goal setting later.

Your passion in life and your life's meaning doesn't always have to be the same as your job. In fact, in some ways, it may be better that it isn't. The thing is that when you're paid for doing something, it often becomes *instantly less rewarding*. Being paid to do something can truly sap the joy out of that thing.

Whatever you do though, the key is to make your passion, the things you stand for, *being true to yourself* your priority.

That might mean shifting around *all* the other factors in your life in order to get there. That might mean choosing a job that lets you work unusual hours, just so you can spend more time doing the things you love.

And you'll now have a tool to help you make every difficult decision in life. Whenever you are faced with multiple options, just ask yourself: which of these things best serves my passion? That will be the meaningful answer.

Follow your passion and you'll always know which way you need to go and what you need to do. EVERYTHING will be truly more meaningful and impactful and you will feel alive in ways that you never thought possible. And when you put all of your heart into something, when you create something of true meaning and value because you're 100% committed to that thing, you will, in fact, end up living forever.

Getting a new set of results from your purpose requires you to rewrite a new game plan. Many times this means resetting the way you look at reality. The biggest achievements often come from efforts or actions that were previously thought to be impossible or irrational. Maybe you are reading this and thinking to yourself "But I've failed in the past" The way too look at this is that failures are only an event, and do not describe a person. Failures and successes are nothing more than data. They are the results to which a particular course of action lead. Embracing failures as learning opportunities, and expressing gratitude for the opportunity to learn from them, boosts self-confidence and leads to greater results in the future.

If you don't think that you are where you are meant to be, you are in good company. In fact, according to a Harris Poll, two-thirds of Americans are unhappy with their life. Most people have not achieved their goals, and are not on track the way that they would like.

That's why the self-help industry is bringing in more than $10 billion a year. People pay exorbitant amounts of money for personal coaching, self-help books, seminars, audio presentations and DVDs to help them achieve their goals, and most of the time, they fail at whatever they are trying to achieve, which puts them right back in the market for self-help.

In the Success habits chapter of this book, I will explore in detail goal-setting and how to use positive focus. Some of the benefits of discovering your purpose and meaning will then become obvious. You will reap the benefits of:

- **Being Able to Define Success:** You will be able to define success, which most people cannot, and often, they have more trouble achieving their goals because they don't know exactly what success is for them. You will not only understand what success means to you; you will also know what successful habits are so that you can create them easily.

- **Replacing Bad Habits with Good Ones:** Instead of learning how to get rid of bad habits, this book will teach you how to replace them with good ones. There is a very specific reason for this, and it has to do with the psychology and hypnosis behind habitual behaviors.

- **Forming Permanent Habits That Will Stick**: You will also find techniques for making habits permanent. Eventually, you want to reach a point where your good habits happen automatically, without you having to think about doing them consciously. These permanent habits are what will carry you along the road to success and the faster and more strongly you can make them stick, the faster you will achieve a higher level of success.

- **Getting the Confidence to be Successful:** People often lack the confidence that they need to be successful and a lack of belief in oneself is one of the main reasons that people fail. This book will demonstrate techniques and tips on gaining that confidence so that you have a foundation for success.

- **Identifying What Triggers Bad Habits:** When you do an action habitually that has negative consequences, it is usually because something triggered it. Both types of habits – positive and negative – have triggers and learning what triggers your bad habits can mean putting a stop to them.

- **Creating Triggers for Good Habits:** Triggers do not just prompt negative habits. You can create triggers for good habits as well. In this book, not only will identifying negative triggers that prompt destructive habits be covered, but also identifying, creating and maintaining good triggers so that positive habits can be developed in their place. These good triggers can then replace the negative ones so that an entire overhaul of your habits takes place, where good habits begin to replace the negative ones quickly and you start seeing real changes in your life.

- **Motivating Yourself to Start the Journey:** In addition to triggers, you will also need motivation, and you will need a great deal of it the first few days that you are working on a new habit – or series of them. You will also learn how to create habits that reinforce each other which adds to your motivation both initially and over the long-term.

- **Motivation to Stay on Track for 30 Days:** 30 days is the key to developing new habits that become deeply ingrained in your subconscious mind. If you can consistently perform an action once a day for 30 days you will be on track to making it a permanent fixture in your life. This book will teach you how to make it through those thirty days, including an entire section on the first few days of the journey, which are going to be the most enjoyable challenge.

- **Overcoming Obstacles that Stand in Your Way:** Finally, you will also get the benefit of expert advice on overcoming any obstacle that stands in your way, whether that be your family and friends being less than supportive, personal issues that make you want to put off your plan for another time and many more, both expected and unexpected, because you will encounter both.

2 SELF DISCOVERY

To a very large extent, many of us tend to see the wrong in others without taking into account or having a close look at ourselves. We subconsciously judge others and not ourselves. Taking a self-assessment is essential in realizing and shaping us to becoming the best version of ourselves. You also need someone who is very honest to help you in your self-assessment.

Usually, the person who can help you is someone whom you can trust. It can be your significant other or a best friend. Also, there are a number of self-assessment tests that you can take for self-discovery on and offline. You can also see a coach or bloody good hypnotist too. Having a mentor is another good idea, either a life coach or someone you can trust that will help you while remaining objective.

Self-assessment involves looking deep into you for an **INSIGHT**. Self-assessment does not mean you are taking some time to reflect on yourself and get to learn about the person you see every time you look in the mirror.

The first step to an accurate self-assessment is to be **HONEST** with you. Take a good look in the mirror and take the time to study the person you see.

Describe the person you see in the mirror using up to a total of **25** *adjectives*. Consider using both positive and negative adjectives. This exercise is important because you are being honest with yourself. Dig deep. Allow for self-discovery.

The next step is to consider your likes and dislikes. This is important to allow yourself to identify the root of your likes and dislikes.

Write down the activities you love doing.

- Which books do you enjoy reading?
- What kind of people do you surround yourself with?
- What are the activities you enjoy during your free time?

Discovering your real self can be scary sometimes. It demands an understanding of your personal aspirations, emotions and even spiritual values. It also involves knowing how best to fulfill the requirements you want in life. If you come to an understanding of all these aspects of life, then you are on the right path to self-discovery.

What we usually focus on in our lives is to make a living, chasing money and we tend to forget the spiritual part of our lives. We neglect the fact that we need to strike a balance between our physical, emotional and spiritual being.

You need to look inside your soul and search for what it needs. It is important to note that we are not just a vessel but instead we have an inner self comprising of the soul which also yearns for satisfaction.

We need to be connected with ourselves and draw attention or move away from distractions from outside. In most cases, our focus is tuned into meeting our external desires.

There will never be a sense of fulfillment if we keep looking at the outside. In most instances, we are busy with the desire to meet the needs of the physical and this causes one to lose him or herself. Take time to perform self-hypnosis. It will help you truly know yourselves better.

Another way to help you discover your real self is by improving your relationship with others. It helps you to place your focus less on material gains and more on intangible values like love and honesty.

We will feel more content when we improve our connection with others by making the people around us happy and helping out where we can. This gives us more of a spiritual satisfaction.

When people embark on a journey of self-discovery, they tend to focus on the physical and emotional side of their personality.

People rarely take into account the importance of spiritual self-discovery. Take some time to explore the spiritual aspect of ourselves. As a result, we will discover a unique and different aspect of our personality we may not even have realized existed.

We are made up of physical, spiritual, intellectual and emotional dimensions. We experience the universe through the individual and collective lenses of these dimensions.

This is not something entirely new.

We know that humanity has always considered these dimensions. We have been informed through Roman and Greek mythology, Roman astrology and ancient religion how spirituality has played an important role in human development.

We perhaps can relate best with moments like witnessing a sunrise or an amazing act of nature that leaves us in a state of awe and wonder, admitting there are things in our life that are beyond our ability to explain and control. We may subconsciously acknowledge the desire to discover this power and it is what we can term "spirituality".

When we talk about spiritual wellbeing, we inevitably think of God. Whoever or whatever we conceive *"him"* to be. Some consider him a supreme being and others consider him as *"the man upstairs"* a father figure. Some may reject the concept of any sort of being, and find their spirituality elements through earth, or in Mother Nature.

So how do we discover the spiritual side of our personalities?

There are various ways of discovering the spiritual side of our personalities. Some people seek spirituality by embracing formal religion; others discover it through yoga or some other form of meditation that enables them to focus on themselves. Others go on a journey of self-discovery and call this a religious experience.

Some have compared this spiritual awakening with a heightened sense of experience. As we consciously allow our inner selves to experience life at a deeper level as compared to what seems obvious around us, we begin to relate to things in a different way.

On the other hand, some of us subconsciously seek help and shelter from a higher being or some of us may refer to as *"god"* when we find ourselves in a dire position. For many people, this moment is also considered a spiritual awakening.

In order to embrace our spiritual side, we need to acknowledge it exists. As we embark on a journey of spiritual self-discovery, we often discover aspects of our personality and our character we have not come across before. Most of us find that it awakens our inner elements and fills a void in our lives.

Some people perceive having faith or spiritual awareness is like following something blindly without proof, as it is intangible. This is common in the early stages of spiritual awakening, where for many people it is an uncomfortable place to be in. But by the end of the day most of us come to accept there are many things in our lives we accept without proof.

When we discover the spiritual aspect of ourselves, we also discover our place in the universe. We often ask ourselves, *"Why am I here"* and *"Where am I heading."* Whatever we call our spiritual reality; these are two fundamental questions we ask ourselves. Spirituality helps us discover the answers to these questions. Spiritual self-discovery can be a journey that fills us with a sense of personal *"completion"* and contentment.

The term *"Self-discovery"* means identifying yourself and your needs. Self-discovery is very important. If you do not discover yourself, and know exactly what you want from life, you have no idea what you are living for.

A step to self-discovery is identifying your needs. Most people are clueless about what they want. To identify your needs, you first need to take a step back and think thoroughly.

Then, when you are in a relaxed state of mind, use self-hypnosis and focus on your thoughts.

Ask yourself questions like what makes you happy, what makes you sad and so on. Along with the question of what, also ask why it makes you feel certain emotions. Seek a deep and strong reason behind it, not a common or general answer.

When you have identified what makes you happy and sad, you can focus on the things that make you happy and stay away from moments that make you sad.

After you have the answer to all of your questions, write them down on a piece of paper so it will be easier for you to view it whenever you need to.

We spend a lot of time looking outside of ourselves in search of happiness. We might feel the happiest when we are under the influence of alcohol or other substances. We might need our family or friends around us to feel happy or we might even think that losing weight or becoming fit is the way to achieve happiness.

Whilst these things may contribute to our happiness, our true happiness lies within us and as we find ourselves, accept ourselves and embrace ourselves only then can we find true happiness that is not dependent on external substances or factors.

This can be one of the most liberating thoughts of all self-discoveries.

Once we learn this fundamental lesson, we determine how we react when things are not going the way we plan. Until that moment, our happiness is mostly dependent on other factors rather than ourselves.

Many people perceive happiness as positive emotions. We associate happiness with feelings or emotions that can range from contentment to pure joy. A lot of us tend to put a lot of expectations on external factors to make us feel those positive emotions.

Until we can come to terms that we are our own source of happiness, it's likely our relationships will never live up to our expectations. They may add to our happiness, but they can never be the source of it. Henry Miller said, *"I have no money, no resources and no hopes, but I am the happiest man alive."*

How do we search for our own happiness?

Happiness is, more about the state of mind as a response to it. To seek happiness within, we first need to change our attitude. We must adopt the mindset that happiness exists within, despite external circumstances.

Perspective is the creator of happiness and it may also be the destroyer of it. Training ourselves to remain positive and content is an important life skill. Once learned, it will help us maintain healthy emotional responses to every situation we face. Self-Hypnosis can be a good way of tapping into the subconscious to understand your inner self. It will help you to answer questions you have related to life.

Self-reflection is important in making or deciding the path in which your life should take. However, you should not be discouraged if you do not seem to get the right answers straight away.

Even though we are all different in terms of gifts and talents, unfortunately not all of us are well aware of what our gifts are. It is also true that most of us know what our strengths are but they do not know how to maximize them.

We also do not know how to use them both for our own benefit and for the benefits of others. *One of the main reasons why people do not maximize their God-given talents is the failure to discover them.* Many young people have the problem of identifying who they really are and what they are in this planet for.

There are a number of questions that you can ask yourself during self-discovery. These questions are:

- Do you still love doing the activities you were doing as a child?

- If you so happen to write a book, what subject would you write on?

- What area or aspect of life you feel you can comfortably help people in?

- What does your close associates, friends or even relatives say about you?

- What is your happiest memory? Search the memory within you and try remembering a certain day that you felt truly happy.

All these questions will lead to the discovery of the **REAL** you.

At the end of the day, you will have personal satisfaction of the direction or path that your life is ought to take.

You will feel motivated and inspired. You will also be more confident about yourself and you can handle anything that comes your way with ease.

Self-discovery is not a thing that happens by itself. Certain situations and factors lead us to discover ourselves. When we grow up, we have to pass through many challenges and setbacks in our lives. These situations make you who you are.

Listed below are some situations that you may face:

1. **Experience** is the most important factor in discovering yourself. You react in a certain way when faced with certain adversities. This is the time you discover yourself. Even if you think in a certain way, your practical actions in that very situation may be entirely different.

2. **Passion** is also a major way to self-discovery. What you are truly passionate about indicates who you are and what your purpose is.

3. **Environment** is another important factor that plays a major role in discovering yourself. The environment in which you are immersed in shapes who you are. If you are in a positive environment, you tend to discover yourself as a person with a positive outlook, and vice versa.

Thus, the elements of self-discovery are transparent and in one time of your life or the other, you get the opportunity to discover yourself. It is important to discover yourself not only for apparent causes, but also for your inner satisfaction.

Do you understand yourself? Understanding yourself assists you in making decisions in life. Often the choices we make without understanding ourselves can be wrong decisions that create further problems. Recognizing our strengths and weaknesses helps us guide our paths to experiences that will provide us with the best possible outcomes of our choices.

If you keep a journal these questions may help you in discovering yourself and to get in touch with your inner thoughts and feelings. These questions can help you make choices in your private life, working life and in relationships.

1. Describe what you believe is truly important in life.

2. Describe what values you uphold in life that best reflects what you believe in.

3. Describe your dreams and what you would want to achieve for yourself in life.

4. Who is your mentor or major influence in your life and how do they help you make decisions? Why are they an important influence?

5. What do you consider your special talents and gifts?

6. What skills would you like to develop in either your personal or working life in the next 12 months?

7. What would you regret not doing if you look back in your life in 20 years' time?

8. What do you consider as your greatest achievement in life?

9. What do you consider as your greatest failure, sadness or disappointment?

Remember there are no right or wrong answers for any of these questions. As you answer them honestly and thoughtfully, the answers will provide you with a picture of who you are and a summary of your hopes, aspirations and the things you can learn from your past choices. Turn your answers into life goals and use them to help make decisions that will shape your future.

The person you look at in the mirror may not be the person you think he or she is. Most of our self-awareness comes from our perceptions of how we think we appear to others. Just how accurate our thoughts about ourselves are, is usually dependent on our life circumstances and the people and events that have shaped our perceptions.

Some people have achieved a sense of acceptance of whom they are and where they fit into the world. For many people, however, the public image they portray to others may not be a true reflection of their inner feelings.

How do people develop negative feelings towards themselves?

Often, they are the result of events where someone we love or trust say or do things that make us feel bad about ourselves. It begins to affect the way we think and feel about ourselves and how we appear to others.

Escaping the negative feelings means learning to love the unique person we are. It also means learning to allow others into our lives again without the fear of hurt or rejection. We can do this alone by subconsciously rejecting the inner voice and countering it with a reminder of all the blessings and successes in our life. Self-hypnosis is an excellent tool for this.

Actor James Baldwin once said, *"I have encountered a lot of people in Europe, I have even encountered myself"*. It raises the question, have you encountered yourself?

To encounter means to meet by surprise or unexpectedly, amongst other meanings. When was the last time you experienced that type of surprise meeting with yourself?

Have you been in a situation where you found out you liked something you didn't think you would enjoy?

You may try new food, or a new sport. Maybe started a new hobby? When this happens without you orchestrating the situation, you are encountering yourself. Many people stay in their comfort zones, and rarely find themselves in a situation where they are challenged by encountering themselves in an unexpected or surprising way.

As a personal challenge, **take time to do something different today**.

Take a walk on the beach or through the forest and use your senses to experience the sights, smells and tastes around you. Walk slowly and keep a journal close.

Allow yourself time to experience things you may usually take for granted and write down the things that you are starting to become aware of. Write about the way they impact you and if they bring back memories or other significant thoughts, write them down as well.

If you are taking a journey of self-discovery, encountering yourself is the first step to learning about the person you are. Another meaning of encounter relates to conflict and confrontation.

Much of the time we prefer not to confront ourselves and we certainly don't want to know the inner conflict, but for self-discovery to be successful, we must be willing to consider even the inner conflicts we have that is constantly raging inside us. We must be willing to confront the unjustifiable fears and assumptions we make, often for no reason.

Sometimes in the course of our lives, we find ourselves saying yes to decisions we later regret. As we think of them, we wonder why we keep allowing ourselves to make the same bad decisions. *Dwelling on the decisions we make can create a cycle of negative thinking.*

We want to be the best partner, or provider for our loved ones, or the best at our job. We want to bake the best cakes or be the best mother or wife. Our self-esteem is often dependent on how others think of us. Our struggle to achieve great things in our life is often the result of a desire to feel accepted by others as a means of feeling self-accepted.

Even the most confident people have their own insecurities.

For instance, celebrities often resort to facelifts and heavy use of makeup to protect their public image. Being insecure does not indicate failure, but it is part of humanity. When those insecurities begin to drive our decisions and our choices, then we risk making poor decisions and creating inner tension and negative self-talk.

To help develop a strong sense of self-acceptance, it is important to ask ourselves about the intentions we have in making our decisions and what our motivations are behind them. Sometimes the good decisions we make are not the best decisions. Instead, they reinforce the cycle of trying to find self-acceptance by the acceptance of others.

Taking an inventory of our own dreams and strengths is essential to breaking this cycle. Our value and worth aren't dependent on what others think of us, but more on how we think of ourselves. As we get in touch with our inner-self and embracing who we are, then we are able to make life decisions that contribute to and enhance our self-image. Most importantly, we have come to terms with who we are.

Self-discovery is greatly dependent on whether you love yourself. Love for oneself is a great asset that one can have in life. First and foremost, you should ask yourself who you are. To a considerable extent, most of us are deeply engrossed on the day-to-day hustles and bustles of life. This entails; making ends meet, running our various businesses and starting new paths for our careers. We are deeply engrossed in this until we forget who we really are. We never stop to discover ourselves.

Always put yourself first and do not look down upon yourself. Loving yourself has nothing to do with ego; it does not mean looking down upon others or being too proud. There's no way you can love others if you do not love yourself first. Thus, loving yourself opens up your life to unique possibilities as you are comfortable in your own skin and is ready to take on anything that lies ahead.

Pure joy is that feeling you felt as a child when you were anticipating opening the presents under the Christmas tree as you woke up on Christmas Morning. It is the feeling you felt as a child when you were faced with what seemed to be the most colorful ice cream you had ever seen.

Do you remember feeling excited as you waited for the gates to open at your favorite theme park?

As we grow older, we lose the sense of pure joy that captivates a child's mind. We rarely let ourselves enjoy our activities with the recklessness we did as children

In your journal, write down 5 childhood memories that you remember that gave you the feelings of deep joy and excitement, both as you anticipated them, and later as you experienced them.

If for example, eating an ice cream on the beach was a special childhood memory that made you skip with joy and anticipation, then take your family or your friends and enjoy ice cream on the beach with them. If you enjoyed going on a trip in your family caravan during holidays, then hire a caravan, take time to go and explore and relive the adventures with your own family.

As adults, the responsibilities of our lives rob us of simple pleasures that give us joy. No journey of self-discovery is complete without looking at the person we were as a child and comparing the person we are now as an adult. The experiences that shaped our personalities are rooted deep within our childhood moments. Spending time reflecting on them is an excellent way to rediscover our inner self.

Personality development is a powerful tool that can really take you to greater heights you never have possibly imagined. Personality development will help you improve on many aspects of your life, which includes; your social health, financial well-being and even emotional health.

Before you get on to personality development, you need first to identify your personality.

- What type of personality are you?

- What are the strong and weak points in your personality traits?

- What are you doing to improve on your weaker traits and what initiatives are you taking to enhance your strong points?

When these questions are honestly answered, you can then move on to the next step, which is the actual personality development. The first thing you need to do for your personality development is to spend some adequate time with yourself. This will help you to be in touch with yourself and you are able to learn more about who you are.

Next, you need to forge the way forward; clearly state the development you want to see within yourself despite your weaknesses and strong points. You need to be realistic and stringent at the same time. Do not be too hard on yourself, as being unrealistic will cause you disappointment. Keep in mind to also not be too soft on yourself, as this will slow down your personality development journey.

Forgive yourself for all the mistakes you have ever committed in life. Trying to do personality development with a grudge and a bitter attitude towards yourself will be useless and will garner no results, as the past hinders your mind and attitude. View all your past failures as a stepping-stone to your future success.

Personality development also demands flexibility. You cannot be rigid and expect personality development to work for you. Be open to whatever requirements personality development has. Be flexible and realistic with your goals as well, because you might need to make some adjustments along the way.

Tune your entire being to personality development, and the journey will be smooth sailing from there. Make it even easier by illustrating what you want to achieve. Picturing or illustrating what you want to achieve helps to keep your progress on track. It is advisable for you to make a daily checklist and set your goals in milestones. This way, you will obtain your goal in a consistent and realistic manner.

We come across many people in life, and they are all different in how they behave, react and reason. All of us are made unique by the different personalities we possess. Therefore, personality is the combination of mannerisms and attributes that makes one person distinct and unique from the other. Personality is formed as a result of many factors.

First, there are personality traits that one inherits from parents and relatives. No wonder you find some of your traits and your likes and dislikes similar to those of your parents or relatives. There are some personality traits that we pick up along the way as we grow and live our lives. As we grow older, we pick up habits, values and beliefs that are dependent on our upbringing. However, the traits we pick up as a child tend to make a lasting impression on us as compared the ones we encounter as adults.

If you want to have successful personality development, you need to be honest with yourself on your personality type. Observe the strengths and weaknesses of your personality type. Do your best to focus and build on your strengths. For instance, if you are talkative and confident, use this to your advantage and let this trait boost your career and ambitions. Also, identify your weaknesses in a very honest and open way. Work on your weaknesses by making deliberate efforts. For instance, if you struggle with pessimistic thoughts all the time, try and find a way to find the positive in things.

There are many ways in identifying your personality type. There are various online personality tests made available for you where the results can be accumulated within minutes.

Personality types are classified into different categories, but generally there are four different temperaments – the introverted and the extroverted, the one who thinks and the one who feels, the one who uses judgment to conclude and the one who uses keenness, and finally, the one who prefers using senses and the one who uses discernment. These different temperaments usually determine how one will react to various situations and the choices one will make.

When you have identified your personality type, you get better understanding of yourself. You are able to maximize your potential and use it to your advantage. For instance, if you are introvert you can channel your talents in ways that suits your personality best.

When you understand your personality type, you will have clarity in your communication with others. You will learn to compliment the other party. For instance, you may be the one who thinks before they act and is very keen as opposed to your friend who uses spontaneity and quick judgment. This creates harmonious relationships.

Everyone has traits that make them unique and that make one David totally different from the other David, though they share the same name. These traits are what sets individuals apart. The environment in which we grow up in and the people we mingle with shapes who we are.

Being honest with yourself is necessary because it will help you to identify your weak and strong points alike so that you are able to use them to your advantage. You can also develop your ability in being a good listener. Listen to others more as opposed to talking to them, and you will be amazed at how much this will help in personality development. When it is time for you to talk, avoid having the *"me"* attitude. Avoid being narcissistic.

Self-discovery is greatly dependent on whether you love yourself. Love for oneself is a great asset that one can have in life. First and foremost, you should ask yourself who you are. To a very large extent, most of us are deeply engrossed on the day-to-day hustles and bustles of life. This entails; making ends meet, running our various businesses and starting new paths for our careers. We are deeply engrossed in this until we forget who we really are. We never stop to discover ourselves.

If you do not love yourself, then there's no way you can love somebody else. Always put yourself first and do not look down upon yourself. Loving yourself has nothing to do with ego; it does not mean looking down upon others or being too proud. There's no way you can love others if you do not love yourself first. Thus, loving yourself opens up your life to unique possibilities as you are comfortable in your own skin and is ready to take on anything that lies ahead.

Do you love yourself?

Most people would probably evade the question, but it is an important and valid question which if we could all answer yes to, would change the way we feel about ourselves and give us self-confidence to achieve the dreams and desires we have for our lives.

It is also about accepting that we have our own special place in this world. Feeling unloved and unworthy is a very lonely feeling. If you cannot find anything to love about yourself, you are probably struggling with self-love.

Learning to love you is possible. To love yourself you must challenge the negative feelings inside that center our thoughts. We must acknowledge that our self-worth and self-acceptance are about the person we are, the person we are comfortable being around when everyone else has left and when we are alone. We must realize that by the end of the day we are all we have.

Take the time to sit and write all the things there is to love about yourself. Be honest with yourself. Do not let toxic thoughts hinder the process. Try to do these five simple things every day and you will find yourself thinking differently:

1. Write down positive qualities you possess and read them aloud to yourself often.

2. Learn to self-care and do something every day that you enjoy. You deserve it!

3. Look in the mirror and learn to love the person looking back at you and tell him or her every day that they are loved and why.

4. Fill your life with people who love you and tell you often what a special person you are. Accept their words and their love without questioning it.

When you have positive affirmations about yourself, you automatically begin to love yourself and you are ready to take up any challenges ahead

Do you know what makes you happy?

If you do, then you have discovered true gold. We are not talking of the momentary flashes of happiness that come when we eat a favorite dessert or drive a beautiful car. These will provide temporary happiness but once the dessert is eaten or the car is returned to its owner, the potential is there for the problems that robbed you of your happiness to return. The happiness being discussed here is the happiness that you can take refuge in, that keeps you at peace with yourself and your world, no matter what is going on around you.

Some people find a sense of happiness in their relationship with God. For some, happiness is found in pursuing a new hobby or learning a new sport. Many define their happiness through their roles in life. However, are these things really the source of true happiness?

Self-acceptance is the key to help us deal with the everyday trials of life. We may express self-acceptance in our relationship with God or with others. However, unless we accept ourselves first, nothing will truly satisfy us or make us happy for very long. Psychologists have long promoted the idea that the greatest love affair we can have is the one we have with ourselves.

Even if we are hit hard by what life may throw at us, it cannot really harm us. We can experience that level of true happiness when we learn to love ourselves and see ourselves as the true gold we are. *We can find refuge in self-acceptance, knowing that we are not defined by our experiences, but rather we can define our experiences by our reactions to them.*

Do you feel you are not good enough?

Everything you do feels like it eventually amounts to nothing so you don't even try?

You find yourself spinning in a downwards spiral because you feel like you don't measure up?

For those who feel this way, this might be their "reality" or truth. Research has shown that the feeling of unworthiness is one of the common contributing factors of weight gain and emotional eating disorders.

We all have room to grow and develop and the most liberating truth of all is that each of us is unique and beautiful. There is no one quite like you on this earth and there never will be.

Once we accept this, we can then focus on ways to improve ourselves. Without appreciating this perspective, it feels as if we are constantly striving to find self-acceptance externally instead of willingly and wholeheartedly accepting ourselves for who we are.

This creates an unhealthy dependency on external validation. A person who only feels happy when people praise him or her will never genuinely feel happy because external praises will die down and is not long lasting. People can't be praising us 24 hours, seven days a week.

So I want you to challenge those thoughts.

Starting tomorrow - **Choose one action to do for you yourself**. It could be as simple as taking that trip to the beach which you have always wanted to or buying that shirt which makes you look good. Give yourself a gift just because. It doesn't need to be fancy if you don't want it to but you

MUST feel the genuine feeling of giving yourself a gift and rewarding yourself. Thank yourself for this far in life you have regardless of the outcome because you know what? You're still alive!

Most people have to battle self-sabotage and rarely say anything nice about themselves but you're not most people and that's why you've picked up this book. You're looking to improve yourself so take this activity seriously for yourself.

You are worth it!

Research shows if we expect good things to happen in our life they often do. Feeling positive isn't some magic formula that guarantees success, but there is a direct linkage between our feelings of positive expectations and the release of endorphins in our brain that act as natural painkillers. This in turn helps to deal with stress and difficulties by thinking with a clearer mind in finding solutions to problems.

The reverse happens when we have low or negative expectations of outcomes. If we think negatively about things, the release of the same endorphins is inhibited.

We tend to feel more depressed and it becomes difficult to think or even consider positive outcomes in a difficult situation. When this cycle of negative thinking continues, it has the potential to become a habit and a strong habit requires a big enough pain in order to break the habit.

The expectations of those around us also influence the expectations of ourselves. This is true for both negative and positive expectations. Teachers and parents who have positive expectations on a student's ability to produce a specific quality of work will encourage students to do better.

A motivated person with high expectations of themselves and a strong belief in what they want to achieve will seek ways to achieve their goals and dreams, which in turn produces endorphins that help to maintain focus even when there are challenges in front of them. Each small success increases the positive expectations and outcomes.

An unmotivated person is weighed down by self-doubt, risks focusing on negative outcomes and expectations and often develops tunnel vision and self-sabotage.

If you are in a state of low self-expectation and negative thinking, surround yourself with positive people who are committed to helping you re-focus and raise the belief in yourself and in what you want to achieve in your life.

The most important question to ask yourself here is do you expect good things to happen in your life?

In the universe, the one highest feeling is love. When you operate with the intention of love, all things feel possible. All things feel bright. The opposite of love is not hate but fear. Fear is a limiting feeling; it makes us operate from a mindset of "not enough", of scarcity. Love, on the other hand, brings courage, determination, understanding and all other positive emotions.

When love is present among people regardless of race or background, there is understanding, peace and progress. The opposite is acts of violence out of fear. Fear of the unknown, of being threatened and of unrealistic fear.

If love alone could be adopted as the guiding principle of individual's lives, there would be no quarrels and divorces between married. There would be no friction between parents and children, no bitterness between friends, and no exploitation of man-by-man.

What are the things others do for you that make you feel loved?

Do you like to have people give you special gifts, or to send you cards and messages assuring you that you are loved and appreciated? Maybe you are the type of person who appreciates a hug as a way of feeling loved, or really enjoy spending time with your spouse or best friend.

The way we give love to others is often indicative of the way we want to be loved ourselves. Most couples enjoy expressing their love to each other. However, many of us have yet to learn a golden lesson.

Often what makes us feel loved is different to the way others give and receive it. Learning what makes our spouse or children feel loved is the key to experiencing deep passionate relationships.

We all enjoy being told we are loved, but for some people, the spoken word is not enough. Telling your spouse or child you love them but never following up on the things that make them feel loved can create feelings of confusion and concern in even the best of relationships.

Learning to recognize the things that make us feel loved and then identifying what the significant people in our lives need to feel loved is a beautiful self-growth adventure that will improve our relationship. It takes little time and effort to learn how to do this, yet as we learn and use this simple technique, our relationships can be transformed.

Ask yourself, what makes you happy? We often spend a lot of our day *"in the pursuit of happiness,"* but do we ever find it or are we on a fruitless road to nowhere when we seek to find it?

Some people try to find money in wealth, others in possessions. Some seek their happiness in their husband or wife or their children. Every day, women around the world go in search of happiness by indulging in *"retail therapy."* For others, that decadent box of chocolates represents happiness. Men might be smiling at those images, yet how many men have to have their night out with the boys or their weekend golf game.

We will try our best to achieve happiness even if it is going to be momentary. *People will let us down; chocolate will make us fat and possessions just never seem enough.* We won't find happiness if we look for it externally. We will never be content unless we first find contentment within ourselves and the world we live in each day.

Here are some thoughts that will help you discover how to be content and achieve happiness:

1. **Don't spend money to find happiness:** You will never be happy if you think money can buy happiness, or that happiness lies in possessions. It just leads to discontentment.

2. **Don't worry about the future:** Your happiness is available to you today. Many people live in hopes that tomorrow they will be happy. Expect happiness to be yours today!

3. **Find your happiness in believing:** Life without belief is a life without hope.

4. **Look at others who are in a worse situation than you and be thankful for what you have:** Contentment and gratitude are the easiest paths to inner happiness.

5. **You need to want to be happy:** Someone wisely said once *"Who does not want to be happy"*

6. **Help Others:** Their pleasure and appreciation will increase your own happiness!

"Don't worry, be happy..." True happiness lies in those four small words. Being happy is a choice, not a pursuit!

When we are worrying about something, it usually shows on our face. We often think we are looking and acting normal, but stress and worry usually manifest itself in some way.

Smiling is often the last thing we feel like doing, particularly in the darkest of times. Yet, when we learn to smile in spite of our problems, we open the door to a new kind of energy that can sometimes bring relief from the pain we are carrying.

Someone once said, *"Smiling is a social obligation."* How many times has your day been brightened by the smile of a total stranger? In that instance, when you instinctively smile back at them you find yourself feeling a little optimistic.

When we smile, our brain releases a hormone that makes us feel good. This immediately lifts our spirit and makes us feel more optimistic. Smiling soon becomes contagious. As we smile at people, often people will smile back at us.

Most people when they feel stressed choose to stay at home because they say, *"they don't feel like socializing."* Instead, go out with family and friends and don't isolate yourself. Likewise, when you are not with your friends, find a hilarious book to read or watch something humorous on television. Laughter produces a positive chemical response in our brain.

Counter negative feelings by focusing on things that will create uplifting thoughts rather than negative ones. Surround yourself with happy people and fun situations. These will help you to think positively about your situations as their own optimism rubs off on you.

Peter Pan was asked by his friend Wendy on how she can fly like him. He replied that to fly, all she had to do was to think happy thoughts. Although this was a children's story and a fictional character, the moral of the story remains true. Thinking happy thoughts may not help us fly, but we can be as happy as we choose to be.

Many people allow their life circumstances to control them. Their sense of happiness rises and falls depending on what is happening in their life. This shouldn't be the case. We can focus on our happiness every day. Happiness is a state of mind, not a reaction to the events in our life.

There are some ways you can help yourself to feel real happiness and you can practice them every day:

1. **Help other people.** As long as your focus is always on yourself, you are aware of things that are not as good as they could be in your life.

2. **Find something to be thankful for every day.** Look around your world every day and find at least one thing to be thankful for each day. Write it down in a journal and review your journal regularly to help you remember the good things in your life.

3. **Surround yourself with good friends.** Happiness is contagious as you should have known by now. As you surround yourself with happy people who are positive, their happiness will affect you and yours will affect them.

4. **Head down memory lane regularly.** Your life is full of happy memories. Write down why those things

made you happy and laugh with someone who remembers them often.

5. **Nurture those you love.** *"How much time do you invest in improving your marriage, or developing your parenting skills?"* Research shows that the happiest people are those with the strongest relationships with their significant others.

6. **Look after your health.** Enjoy yourself running around with the children, doing Zumba at the gym or playing golf with your mates. Looking after your health fills you with energy and when you add laughter to the fun you are the winner!

7. **Try something new you have always wanted to do.**
Set yourself a challenge to do something new every week no matter how much you feel you can't do it. Have a go and enjoy the experience. You may find yourself surprised by the results.

8. **Don't expect too much.** Keep your expectations on yourself and others at a reasonable level. If you set the standard too high, you are setting yourself for disappointment. Accept and appreciate the things that people do for you.

Happiness is within our reach if we focus on achieving it. Appreciate the good things in our life and the gift of love that is given to us by our significant others. They are the things that remain constant when other things in our life are not going as well. They help us keep the difficult moments we will inevitably face in perspective and give us hope when things around us may seem hopeless.

The subconscious mind plays a major role in how we perceive and project ourselves. When you positively utilize the subconscious mind, then it can bring a huge advantage to your life and will absolutely change your life for the better. The subconscious mind is the place where your emotions and feelings lie, therefore having a positive subconscious mind possesses the power to reverse negativity.

We often have conversations with ourselves on a daily basis. At times it creates an internal struggle between the different *"voices"* we often hear when these conversations occur.

These conversations are known as self-talk. Our subconscious is constantly *"talking"* to us and often answering itself at the same time. The voices we hear and the decisions that arise from our self-talk can potentially help us make important decisions. But how much can we rely on our subconscious and our self-talk?

Perception can be altered by the current state we are in. Identifying whether the self-talk is based on facts or perceptions will help us make a better decision using our subconscious mind.

The mind has the ability to project imagination. You are in control of what you want and it takes place in your subconscious mind. This process is what makes a person motivated to achieve their desired success.

A positive attitude leads to a happier state of mind. Whilst negative attitude tends to miss all beautiful things that life has to offer. One of things you might be doing unintentionally is constantly bemoaning over your failures.

Emotional well-being is one of the most important gifts we can give to ourselves. Doing regular emotional checkups and ensuring we do something to aid our emotional well-being is essential to maintaining a healthy life.

Each of us has developed a set of values that determine how we think and feel about life, including the right and wrong behaviors. When we see other's doing things that are outside our acceptable behavior parameters, we usually react in a negative way.

Learning to accept the 'what is wrong to us may not be wrong to others', is an important part of personal development. We may not agree with their choices, but we respect and allow people to be themselves. They have values and ideas that may differ from yours.

We act the way we do mostly because it often originated from our childhood experiences. Like, we have been told to eat with our mouth closed. To us, it is a manner that we consider important to ourselves and our families to try and achieve. So when we interact with people who have not been taught of such rules, it is inevitable for us to be frustrated with them. Often, our values and behaviors become the measure for everyone else's behavior.

If you could take a photo of your life today and then zoom in on something special or important, which part of your life would you choose? Would it be something that is causing you distress or the opposite? If your still picture was a movie, what title would you give it? Would you like the experience to continue or do you wish it had never happened? If you could relive this part of your life again, would you? If not, why wouldn't you?

Imagining our life as a movie or a photograph is a good way of examining our life further. When we give important life experiences a name, we can focus on the important events in our life and especially on the ones that continue to influence us today.

Have you ever noticed when you take a wide angled shot of a scene you see a lot of picture but very little detail? Even if you zoom in on one part of the picture that interests you, you miss out on the bigger picture.

We often look at life in this way. We look at the big picture and forget the details that bring beauty and interest to our lives. We are at risk of losing a range of perspective if we only look at life from a single point. We need perspectives to understand our life experiences and its purpose.

Revisit your photographed memory again. How different does the picture look close up and how does it look at a distance? If the picture is distressing, close up, try to zoom back and look at the picture from a distance to give you a bigger perspective. Does it change the picture at all?

So you see, if we focus on our life from a distance, we forget to appreciate the individual and smaller things that make life unique.

We cannot begin to act and think positively until we have learned to experience and deal with our feelings, without being pulled down by them. Most people are led by their *"gut instincts"* when making decisions.

We are always surrounded by beauty. The challenge is whether we allow ourselves to see it because life can be very distracting especially if you live a fast-paced lifestyle. If ever you feel stuck, take a pause to be inspired by your surroundings.

Some of the greatest paintings of all times were inspired by nature. "Irises" by Van Gogh, painted in 1889 was inspired by simple flowers. The thing is that these inspirations are free and ready for you to access it whenever you so choose. The key is to be present.

Here is an effective way to be more present and it is the art of doing things slowly, deliberately and more subconsciously.

1. Prepare a bowl of mixed nuts in front of you. You can do this at any time of the day.

2. When you are ready, slowly reach out to select any nut and bring it close to you. Feel free to feel and analyze the texture. You can do whatever you want with it.

The goal is to understand and focus your awareness to that single nut fully.

3. Next, put the nut slowly into your mouth but don't chew it yet. Taste the nut in your mouth first before you chew and when you chew, do it slowly. Focus on finding the taste of the nut instead of the act of chewing.

4. Allocate at least 10 to 15 minutes for this exercise. You may feel the need to rush through something as simple as eating nuts but refrain from doing so. Rushing through it defeats the purpose of this presence exercise.

What you will find at the end of this exercise is the discovery of joy in something as simple as eating a single nut. You would be surprised at how much taste and aroma can come from something simple when we bring our focus and awareness to the current act. You may feel that this is something trivial but hey don't take my word for it. Try it out and see for yourself.

Don't miss out on the simple joys.

The law of attraction in our lives has become *"the thing"*. Everyone wants to apply *this law* in their everyday activity. This is because all of us have dreams and we would want these dreams to come true someday.

Most of us want a very successful life with plenty of achievements and happiness. We all want to have our desires to come true. Therefore, the law of attraction helps us to tune our minds and feelings to draw the lifestyle that we want.

Here are steps to activate the Law of Attraction

The first thing to do is to describe the type of life that you want and be able to see it in your **mind's eye**. When you want something, you should ask from the cosmos and you should also have a picture of what it is. Recognition of your dreams and requirements first begin with forming a mental image of whatever you want. Visualization is very important because you can involve both your conscious and your subconscious mind. When you do this visualization process, it is important that you feel as if you already have it.

The next part is to think positively. If you are negative, the Law of Attraction cannot be activated. If you want to achieve the success that you want, then you must be positive. Always think that there are different ways to achieve a goal. Positively affirming yourself is the most important thing.

You should also always be thankful and be willing to share the things that you have. This way, you will be able to attract more. Always look at what you have and not what you do not have.

Now, how do you feel about yourself today? Do you think that if you could just lose weight you would feel happy and perfect? Do you wish you had enough money to buy the hot new car that will make you the envy of your mates?

For many of us, our physical images and possessions help define what we think of ourselves. Unfortunately, that is a shoddy way of thinking and that seems like we are living in the future rather than in the present.

When this attitude of *"life will get better when something happens"* affects the way we live our life, we need to challenge those thoughts. If we don't love ourselves now, we potentially can keep on looking to what the future might do to help us to improve ourselves. We need to embrace the person we are now and see that the better resources are already inside us.

Unless we want to lose weight for ourselves, our weight loss attempts probably won't be successful. We can hinder our own development and achievements if we try to live in the future. By embracing the opportunities we have today, we are more likely to achieve our goals and ambitions in the future.

Our self-worth is not dependent on what we do. Unless we learn to enjoy and appreciate the person we are, we are more likely to bash our achievements.

The danger of this approach is that if we fail in our expectations, it undermines the way we think about ourselves. Our self-esteem remains weak and we usually feel less incentive to keep trying new things. If we base our self-worth on accepting ourselves as we are today, every achievement can be celebrated.

Ask yourself; ever had anything major happened in your life? When these things happen, especially when we feel betrayed or let down by people we love, it's easy to feel that we can never trust people again. The effect of one or two negative things in our life can cause us to spiral down on a path of seemingly no return. We may even lose confidence in our own ability to make good decisions.

Being stuck in the past and letting the past manipulate and dictate the future is a major reason many people feel that their life does not progress. That is why **ACKNOWLEDGING** it is the first stage of healing and progression towards a new tomorrow. Remember, no matter what changes that is heading your way, always remember your self-worth.

If you recognize that some incident in the past is affecting your present actions, it is wise to seek professional help or the leader of your religious group if you have faith in God. There are also some other things you can do to help yourself.

1. The past is the past and nothing that can be said or done will change what has happened. Having acknowledged that maybe the past is causing us to have negative thoughts, we can change them to positive ones by focusing on a new beginning.

2. Challenge yourself to see yourself not as you were in the past, but as you want to be in the future. Write down how you want life to look like ten years from now and write it as if it was a reality.

Read it regularly and see how it changes. You'll be surprised at the result.

All of us face change in our life. Sometimes we look forward to it and enjoy the preparations that are involved in making it happen. On other occasions, change can be very distressing. Usually occurring without warning and we are usually unprepared for it. We can feel quite disorientated when change is unexpected and it can produce physical reactions we may feel we have little control over.

Facing unplanned change with a prepared mind helps to re-orientate life even when it seems to be out of our control. If we accept that change is inevitable, we see the sense in thinking about and preparing to deal with it well ahead when it actually happens. It also helps us to reflect on how we will deal with our responses when faced with stress and change.

Taking the time to plan and prepare for change is not inviting fate, but facing reality. People who work in occupations that involve dealing with sudden unexpected emergencies are in a state of readiness at all times. They learn to anticipate all possible scenarios by learning how to deal with them before they occur. They learn how to prevent or minimize the damage.

We gain valuable insight into how to prepare for change by learning how to apply their approaches to potential change and stressful situations. We prepare for change, or potential stresses in three ways:

1. Firstly, the higher the risk of something happening, the more we should anticipate it likely to happen. People living in areas where there is a considerable risk of a natural disaster occurring, prepare for its inevitably, by preparing their surroundings each year and psychologically being ready for it.

2. Contrary to what people may think, being psychologically prepared for change is possible. Although it is impossible to know what it will be like as a parent, for example, we can prepare ourselves by reading and identifying possible areas of concern we may personally face in our new parenting role.

3. Thirdly, we can also learn to manage our responses and thoughts in times of minor changes and challenges. As we do this, we are providing ourselves with invaluable training. Learning how to deal with the many minor challenges and changes we face daily, will help us to develop the skills to deal with the unexpected major ones.

Always remember. There is potential in you. All your virtues and power are waiting for you to manifest and use to fulfill your existence. No matter where you are, who you think you are and the circumstances you are in; you have all the right to accomplish your goals. Every single human being is worth every ounce of success the world has to offer.

When you start to implement all the goodness this book has to offer, all your fears and insecurities will begin to disappear.

What replaces them are courage and knowledge. They are your sidekicks to go through that wonderful journey with you.

All you need to do is start with that very first step. Every journey starts with the visualization of your dream. From there, you need to grab on to your faith and belief. Slowly but surely, they will help carve the path to your success.

The last thing that you need to do is take massive action!

3 TAKE CONTROL OF YOUR MIND

Do you ever get the feeling like you're constantly putting out fires? Like life is one massive struggle to stay afloat? Do you come home from work feeling tired and stressed and without the energy to do anything other than collapse in front of the TV? Do you always feel like you're just not quite as happy as you think you could be/should be? That's life my friend. Or at least it's life as many of us have come to know it. In fact, though, there's no reason that this should necessarily be the case. The problem is that we're always chasing after the gold at the end of the rainbow and in doing so, we never stop to smell the roses. I have been guilty of this in the past, but these days I recognize that I actually only do exactly what I want to do that either helps my brand, or makes me feel better.

We're sometimes never happy because we're always striving for what's next. We're always stressed about what's coming up and we never appreciate what we have until we lose it. We think that the only way to change this is to change our lives.

We need to change the way we think about our situation and we need to change the way we approach life's problems and the way we enjoy the moment and that means taking control of our minds. Everything we do first starts with a thought process; we don't see the world around us, we actually think it. Thoughts are so powerful and as a hypnotist, I know that if I can change someone's thoughts, I can basically change and enrich their lives when they come to see me. Once you can change the way you think, you can take back control and you can feel confident, relaxed and happy in the exact same circumstances. Once you can do that, you can start creating the space to actually plot a course and to start changing life for the better. You can stop treading water and start swimming. All very abstract, yes. So far it sounds like a platitude from a bumper sticker.

Think about it this way: it's not the situation that matters, it's your perception of the situation that matters. Think about it this way: you can be surrounded by fire and be completely calm and happy, or you can be relaxing at home and be completely stressed.

In the first case scenario, you're surrounded by fire but you believe that you're invincible. As far as you're concerned, nothing can hurt you and you have nothing to fear. As a result, you remain calm and your heart rate doesn't even rise (well, other than from the effects of the heat!).

In the second scenario, you're sitting at home, comfortable and with a warm cup of tea. You're surrounded by family or even in my case just a dog who love you and you have the

TV on showing your favorite TV program. But all you can think about is the work you have to do tomorrow, your money problems and the fact that you're not as well off as successful as you'd like to be.

As a result, your body and brain interpret the signals as you being in danger. Your brain produces more norepinephrine, more cortisol, more dopamine and more adrenaline. As a result, the person who is surrounded by flames but deluded is actually happier and calmer than the person who is sat at home but stressing out.

Now, of course, I'm not saying that you should be like the deluded person surrounded by fire… That's dangerous!

But you also really shouldn't be like the stressed person who should be relaxed. And here's the thing: lots of us are!

THIS is why it's so important to start taking control of your mind. Because it's what will impact on your happiness, your calm, your focus and on all the other things that contribute to you being happy and successful.

Changing your environment and circumstances is often incredibly difficult – but you can change your mind today. And that can bring incredible benefits.

Imagine that you have a very stressful day and you've been working hard on a massive to-do list. You need to make lots of calls, manage your work team and just generally deal with a lot of fires. Plus, you have a date tonight with someone that you think will be awkward and you have pressing, on-going money concerns. Sound familiar?

Anyway, you're on the bus or in the car going from one meeting to the next and in that time there is no benefit to being stressed. In other words, you can carry on worrying about all those things you have to do if you want to… but it's not going to do you any good. What would be far preferable, would be if you use this short amount of time as a break in order to recuperate.

You can put yourself in a self-hypnotic state and become indifferent to that stress. You can sit back and just clear your mind. Now, when you arrive at your meeting, you're going to be much more recharged and energized because your brain has had the opportunity to get some rest. The result is that you'll feel much better and you'll work much more efficiently as well.

If you get really good at self-hypnosis, then you can eventually start to employ 'waking state' now, you're going to be in a relaxed, focussed state at the same time as walking, talking and doing other things. You'll be impervious to stress because you've learned to control your mind and control your emotions.

Because you aren't giving your concerns the emotional weight that you may have done in the past, your brain isn't activating the 'salience network' that it uses to respond to threats and you're able to just carry on going about your business in a completely calm and efficient manner!

Self-Hypnosis is one way to stop worrying about all those little nagging concerns and doubts and to start focussing on your body and your senses a little more. I cover self-hypnosis later in this book for you and strategies and exercises for its use.

The fact of the matter is that most of us are so in our own heads that we barely notice half of what's going on around us. We walk in a dream state worrying about work, or about our relationships and we hardly take the time to stop and smell the roses – literally or metaphorically.

Try this right now. Turn off any music that you're listening too and instead just start to notice the sounds around you. Really listen! What can you hear? Perhaps the hum of traffic outside? Maybe the murmur of conversation in the room? Maybe you can hear next door?

Or perhaps you're outside? Maybe you can hear the sound of birds?

Likewise, you can probably smell a whole load of things you hadn't noticed. And if you take a moment to feel your own body, then you can probably notice the sensation of the seat pushing into your legs and into your buttocks. Maybe you can feel the blood filling your face and making you feel hot. Or perhaps there's a cool wind blow against you. What direction is it heading?

Likewise, listen to the sounds of your own breathing and feel your abdomen expand and shrink as you do.

Once you do this, you'll find that you stop worrying what's going on around you and that you start to appreciate your environment a little more. There's so much that you normally miss!

You can try doing this on walks too. Go for a walk with no music, no phone and nothing else and try just being present and noticing the world around you. It's a calming and invigorating experience at the same time!

Practicing this is important because as with practicing self-hypnosis, it will eventually become something that you can just engage at will. Now you can choose when you want to start listening better to what people are saying to you and when you want to really focus on the day out you're having with your children.

Again, you can leave your work concerns at home.

And try focussing on the sensations of your body more the next time you're intimate with a sexual partner. Don't worry about your technique, what you're going to do next, whether they like you… instead, really focus on how the touch of their hand feels on your body. You'll find that you instinctively know what to do next and that you start to be much more passionate and responsive. You'll become a better lover, simply by getting out of your own head. And you'll feel it far more forcefully.

This is true for everything else as well. Next time you have a bath, take a moment to really appreciate the warmth and the softness of the water against your skin. Indulge yourself in the smell!

The next time you eat cereal in the morning, remind yourself how much you enjoy that cereal and how happy you are not to be going to work.

This is what so many of us don't do. So many of us are constantly in a dream state and worrying about other things that we actually miss what's going on around us.

Being stressed and having no control over your mind is doubly problematic – because not only does it make us unhappy directly but it also distracts us from the things going on around us all the time that could be making us happier.

Remember what I just said about the importance of focussing on what's going on around you? And on being awake, alive and in the moment? Chapter one discussed "Getting That Passion"

The question you might now be wanting to ask is: why is it so hard to obtain the same focus and connection with the world that comes naturally to infants?

There are lots of answers to that question but one of the most pertinent is that we are too set into our routines and we aren't stimulated enough.

Try that exercise again where you listen to your surroundings. What can you hear? Can you hear a ticking clock somewhere?

There's a good chance that the answer is yes if you're indoors but you might not have noticed it until I asked you to listen to it. And why not? Because you've become desensitized to it.

What's happened is that your brain has heard that ticking before. It's the exact same every second and it's something you're completely used to. As such, your brain says 'this isn't important' and it pushes it into the background.

Meanwhile, the worries that are flooding through your mind constantly seem very important.

The same thing happens if you cut ping pong balls in half and place them on your eyes. When you do this, you'll at first see the insides of those ping pong balls, as you would expect. But after a few minutes, things will go fuzzy.

Why? Because nothing is changing. The nerve endings in your eyes have become tired of the exact same stimulation and so they're turning off. Nothing is moving, nothing is changing – it's inefficient for them to keep firing.

This is called the 'Ganzfield' experiment and it's quite interesting if you ever want to induce hallucinations naturally.

Now think about what you do in your daily life:

- You walk the same route to work
- You take the same ride on the same bus

- You have the same breakfast
- You have the same conversation with the same people
- You perform the same tasks throughout work
- You get home and sit in the same place

People... this is killing us. Our brain has a complete lack of stimulation and excitement from this kind of activity. We evolved to be constantly moving, constantly in danger, tracking our prey through the wild... and when that happened everything around us seemed important, dangerous and salient.

But now, we're sleepwalking through life. Everything is safe and everything is the same...

If you want to be more present and more in-the-moment, then you need to submit yourself to environments and situations that are exciting, novel, different and interesting.

If you do this, then you'll automatically forget all those things that are making you stressed. You'll automatically become more engaged with the world and less worried about your own petty concerns.

So take different routes home from work.

Learn new skills and hobbies.

Have conversations with strangers.

Try new foods.

When you do, your brain will light up and come alive and you'll get a reprieve from your money and relationship problems. Better yet, you'll form new neural connections which will once again help you to become sharper, smarter, faster, more creative and more alive.

So the best type of mental state is the one that lets you switch to other mental states at will. Our aim is to be in control of our brains and our thoughts and to be able to switch from one state of mind to another with ease.

In other words, all types of thought and all types of mental state are important, valid and helpful.

Except one.

What is that one? It's the one where you're just incredibly distracted by all the constant demands being placed on you.

And this is where the 'modern ache' starts to come in.

Earlier, we learned how we were desensitized to much of the natural stimuli coming into our minds through our senses. We take the same route to work and do the same things every day and as a result, we are very much desensitized to everything around us.

The problem is: our modern culture is all too aware of this and it tries to exploit it.

While you're happily mulling over the day's events you see, you're also being distracted by:

- Bright billboards and adverts
- Your phone's constant buzzing
- The TV
- The radio
- Your boss emailing your
- Cars honking their horns
- Alarms

All these things are designed to grab our attention and to over stimulate us so that they can get us to spend money/work/pay attention.

And this is what's killing our ability to focus, relax and concentrate as much as anything else.

Do you know why alarms are designed the way they are? They make a beeping noise because it's something we would never hear in the wild. As such, it's strange and unusual to our brain and it sits up and takes notice – in comes that salience network and in comes that cortisol, norepinephrine and general stress.

And this is what wakes most of us up in the morning! We're startled awake from complete, deep sleep by a loud 'alien' sound.

Then what do we do? Normally, we will check our phones.

Bright light = even more cortisol (the stress hormone) being produced in our brains.

Then looking at adverts starts to grab our attention because that's what they're designed for.

Then we read our email. What's this? A message from your boss asking if you can do something for them as soon as you get in?

Now you're stressed and focussed on that. And thus, as you do your teeth it's all you can think of.

Then we sit down and instead of doing the things we need to do first, we start our day by doing that thing that we were asked to do. Now we're in a 'reactive' state of mind and we're not able to do what's most productive or most important for us.

And so it continues for the rest of the day. We're constantly being tugged in every direction by computers, work, money problems, adverts, games, texts… and that's using up all our ability to pay attention, to focus and to think.

So is it any wonder that you're struggling to start focusing? Or that you're so 'wired and tired' all the time? Or that you're struggling to stay on top of things?

Using self-hypnosis to gain focus will really help with this because it will give you the ability to control your focus and your ability to concentrate. Now you can say 'no' to worrying about that email. And you can say 'no' to focussing on the TV ads. And you can engage with your body and mind whenever you want in order to recharge and in order to start enjoying the world around you.

What's also really good though, is if you can reduce all that noise, distraction, stimulation and chatter. This will just make everything easier for you and will help you to better focus on the things that matter to you.

One example of how you can do this is with your 'morning ritual'.

A morning ritual is basically a series of steps that you will endeavor to go through every single morning before you leave the house/start with work. This lets you stop being reactive and start being proactive. It means that you're now setting the pace and deciding how you want to begin your day – and it can help to make you more productive and efficient for the entire day that follows.

So what might a morning ritual look like?

Some great things to add:

- Catch up on the news in a way that doesn't require the TV!
- 10 minutes of self-hypnosis
- No phone/email/computer until you get to work
- Do some exercise – 10-20 minutes is better than nothing and a great way to give yourself a surge of energy

- Healthy breakfast

- Write a to-do list – now you're taking control of how you're going to spend your morning/day instead

- Take a cold shower – it doesn't have to be cold but if you have the willpower to try it, you'll find it invigorates you, wakes you up and really helps you to focus and feel your own body

- Pet the dog or groom him/her

Similarly, you can also try introducing an evening routine. There are a few things this can help with:

- Write a journal – writing a journal is a great way to reflect on the day and how it could have been better/what you enjoyed about it

- No TV or phone for 30 minutes before bed – this will help to get your brain ready for sleep and will increase your production of the sleep hormone melatonin

- Read in bed – again, this helps you to feel sleepier and is also very meditative

- Have a warm bath – this can help relax the muscles for better sleep

- Lay out your clothes and/or gym kit for tomorrow

The start of creating a controlled mind and gaining that increase in focus, is to identify the way you feel and what you're thinking when you're doing something…

Say you're afraid of public speaking and you want to try and get rid of that phobia forever. The first thing you would do is to be more mindful and to listen to your own thoughts and reflect on them. If you've been practicing, this should rob them of their power as you become detached and aloof from those thoughts.

But at the same time, you're also going to make a note of them so you can try and change them…

Another technique used for the same end is 'journaling'. This involves writing down the feelings as they come to you, or writing them in a journal at the end of the day. That evening routine is coming in handy at this point! I have created an excellent Hypnotic Goals Planner journal you can purchase for this, right from Amazon.

Thought challenging is simple: it means that you're looking at those thoughts you made a note of and now you're challenging them and testing whether or not you really think they're true.

So if you're afraid of public speaking, it may be that you think things like 'I'm going to stutter and everyone will laugh at me!'.

In thought challenging, we're going to deconstruct that belief and see if it really is likely/if it is anything to really be afraid of.

Ask yourself:

- Why would you stutter? Do you normally stutter when you talk?

- Why would people laugh at you? Are people usually that unkind?

- Would you laugh if someone had a hard time giving a speech? Or would you be more sympathetic and understanding than that?

- Does it matter? You aren't going to see these people again… why does it matter what they think of you?

Ask yourself these things and focus on the fact that the worst case scenario really isn't all that bad. Once you can start doing that, you'll see that there's nothing to be afraid of. You can even repeat a maxim to yourself as a 'positive affirmation':

"It really doesn't matter what these people think of me. It really doesn't matter what these people think of me."

This is a great change because a lot of us are so caught up in everything that's wrong, that we never think about how much is right.

Take a moment at the end of each day and write down the things you are grateful for. Your partner maybe? Your job? Your house? Your dog? The binge watching show you love to watch? There's so much to be happy about but a lot of the time we miss it. Take your new ability to change the way you think and focus on it. Suddenly everything becomes happier.

4 GET AND STAY MOTIVATED

The first thing you need to do to improve your ability to focus and stay motivated is to ensure that you remove distractions that can override your dorsal attention network. This means you need to create a working or even rest environment that will be free from distractions and that makes you as comfortable as possible.

But we need to go further than this if we're going take complete control over our motivation. Ideally, we need to ensure that our ventral and dorsal attention networks are aligned. How do we do this?

The answer lies with the reason that we are distracted in the first place. The reality is not just that we think other things are more important, but also that we feel that what we should be doing isn't important. You might know subconsciously that you need to clean the house, go to the gym or tidy up. That's your dorsal network doing its work.

But your body doesn't know that. To your body, this is an un-stimulating activity that isn't serving any of your prime directives. One thing our brain needs is stimulation and that corresponds with neural activity that comes from doing something that seems biologically important. This is why we find it easy to focus on Facebook or films – they simulate exciting, important events happening, all charged with emotion.

Entering information into a spreadsheet though? Not so much.

But our human intelligence comes from our ability to focus not just on what is biologically important right now but on what we need to be doing in the distant future. In other words, it's our ability to extrapolate, plan and predict that has made us so highly effective.

This comes from our working memory, which is our ability to store information in our 'mind's eye' as it were. We can focus on things that have happened or that we think are going to happen and this causes the brain to light up as though they are happening. This is what our visualization really is – we're internalizing our experience so as to be able to manipulate the variables.

One way to give yourself more motivation then, is to learn to link the boring event or the thing you don't want to do, to the worthwhile and important goal that you hope to achieve.

In other words, you need to remind your brain why you are doing this using visualization. If you're sitting typing out a spreadsheet, visualize how this is going to eventually lead to you being wealthier, more successful in your career and less stressed tonight. Consider what will happen if you don't do it – you will be behind with work or rest and you won't be able to accomplish the goals you're aiming for!

If you're struggling to motivate yourself to go to the gym, then imagine what it will be like to have ripped abs and a 10% body fat. Seem worth it now?

Another tip is to make whatever you're doing more interesting and more fun if you can, which makes it more salient to your brain. I always say that the best cure for writer's block, in particular, is to make the scene or the paragraph you're writing more interesting. If it's not interesting enough to write, then it likely won't be interesting to read!

If you're in performing data entry, then make it a little more rewarding by putting some music on in the background – as long as it isn't too distracting to prevent you from paying attention to what you're doing. I cover multi-tasking later and how the brain can only really focus on one thing at a time, Oh, and once you get into the flow – make sure that there is nothing there to break that concentration.

Procrastination is one of your biggest obstacles to achieving what you want to achieve. So many of us have things we want to accomplish that we never manage to fulfill. Too often, this is mainly down to a lack of concentrated, strategic effort.

So, we maybe blame time. We might claim that we would love to start our own business/improve our home/write a novel/get in shape/actually clean the kitchen... but we just don't have the time because we are so busy with work.

This is simply untrue.

24 hours (16 of which are spent awake) might not sound like that much, but it should be *more* than enough to accomplish all you hope to.

After all, didn't you watch a whole marathon of your favorite TV show only last month on Netflix?

Didn't you spend over an hour watching TV or browsing Facebook *most evenings* last week?

If you were to have spent all that time in a way that was useful and productive, then of course you would have accomplished your goals. And probably *much much more*. Heck, you would probably speak five languages right now!

Part of the problem comes down to procrastination. But really this is a result of some much bigger issues: those being energy and discipline. In this guide, you're going to learn to solve *all* of those problems.

Procrastinations comes from a lack of discipline. This is what happens when you sit down to get some work done and immediately your mind begins to wonder.

This, in turn, comes down to a couple of factors. For starters, the work you need to do is likely somewhat boring and unrewarding. If the work you had to do involved playing a computer game or eating a delicious pie, you probably wouldn't procrastinate.

The other problem comes down to stress and anxiety. When we feel anxious and stressed, our mind wants to turn to the source of that stress and focus on that – it doesn't *allow* us to engage in the things we need to do. This is why we'll often find ourselves killing time by browsing the web: it's a little like burying your head in the sand and hoping the problem will go away.

Of course, the irony is that delaying will only make matters worse!

Ultimately, this is an example of you *not being in control of your own mind*. This is the 'monkey mind' at its worst and it's a great example of how we can feel out of control when it comes to where we want to direct our energy.

And that brings us to the other problem: energy.

Often, we are simply too tired to do the thing that we need to do. Perhaps you've just had a long day in the office and now you need to tidy up or clean the hoes. You're too tired to do that and so you think you should give yourself five minutes to rest first. Which quickly becomes ten minutes, or twenty. And then it's bedtime.

Sometimes we lack energy and determination to such a degree that we can actually procrastinate before it's time for bed! We actually find ourselves watching rubbish TV or browsing Facebook when all we want to do is sleep – because we can't face the thought of having to get up and brush our teeth.

And energy is responsible for this in a bigger way too. You see, discipline actually *requires* energy. Whenever we make any choice, making the harder choice actually requires energy. This is why we also tend to become *less moral* as it gets later in the day. Our determination is fatigued at this point and so we'll often take the easy route

Now you know all of this, the next question is how you can go about ending that procrastination and gaining unstoppable motivation.

Motivation and discipline are actually two sides of the same coin and this is an area of your life that you should look to cultivate if you want to become a more impressive, powerful and successful version of you.

Discipline ultimately comes down to control over your own emotions and actions. And that, in turn, means you need to learn to stop being a *slave* to the way you feel.

We don't want to work through the night because it doesn't feel nice. And so we do it slowly and our mind fights us every step of the way.

The disciplined individual, however, can simply tell themselves that it doesn't matter whether they like it: it has to be done and that is that. They choose one goal, one objective and they shut out *all* other distracting thoughts and impulses.

This is powerful stuff because it allows you to gain laser focus over what you are doing and to complete any task. At the same time though, it also creates congruence in everything you say and do. People will notice that you are not easily upset by things people say, desperate to please them, or torn about what to do: you are decisive, disciplined and immune to life's concerns.

This is *so* important. So often we try to please everyone because we want to be liked and we end up making weak decisions that end up upsetting everyone. So often we let our emotions lead us in our conversations and disputes which causes us to react badly in conversation. And so often we curl up in a ball and don't do the things that need to be done, which only causes our life to become more difficult.

The disciplined person rises above this and they are in *complete* control over their actions and reactions.

How do you gain discipline?

The same way you gain anything else: through practice and training.

And what this also means is that you need to recognize the discipline that exists in every moment. Discipline is the conscious choice to focus on one thing and to shut out distractions. Distraction *is* procrastination and procrastination is distraction.

So, when someone is talking to you in a conversation, it is your job to focus acutely on what they're saying.

When you are meant to be working in the office but you're interested in what is happening on the other side of the room, it is your job to *ignore* that urge to look up.

When you are trying to exercise but you feel tired, it's your job to ignore the feeling and to power on through anyway.

It starts with recognizing that your feelings don't matter. As long as you're not hurting yourself, it doesn't matter if you're a little hungry, a little bored, a little cold, a little tired. It doesn't matter if you feel you deserve a treat. Being an adult is all about resisting that urge and on focussing on the things that you need to focus on in order to accomplish your goals.

This is a kind of 'incidental' training that turns all of your interactions and experiences into chances to hone your focus and discipline. But you can also set up further training opportunities throughout your routine.

One example might be to take a cold shower. Standing in a cold shower takes a huge amount of determination and discipline and this is something your body and mind will fight you on every step of the way. But if you can force yourself into that cold water anyway, you will be training and harnessing your determination. And actually, cold showers are very good for us seeing as they help us to produce more testosterone, they increase blood circulation and they train our immune systems.

Another example is to make your bed. This is something very simple but it's a great habit to get into: if you can successfully motivate yourself to make your bed every morning, even when you're stressed, even when you're in a hurry, then this will be great training to get yourself to do *other* things that you need to.

The Importance of Reward

I'm really not telling you to become a monk here. While it's important to be disciplined and to fight procrastination, it's *also* important to enjoy life. And no one is going to be 100% disciplined 100% of the time – no matter what they tell you. Being too repressed and too strict can end up leading to more serious issues down the line.

What I'm telling you to do instead, is to give yourself rewards at *set times* and only once you have worked for them.

Want to eat a big chocolate bar? Sure you can. But only once you've gone a whole day keeping your calorie total to X amount.

Want to kick back and enjoy a good Richard Barker book? That's fine. But first, you need to complete X amount of work so that you've got that under your belt.

Giving yourself rewards for good behavior is a great way to motivate yourself and to allow you to add a little fun to your life *without* having to completely give up on being disciplined and strict.

One simple example of this might be with your daily work. If you normally start your day's work by getting a cup of tea and then having a chat, it's time to turn that on its head. From now on, you get the cup of tea and the chat as a *reward* for doing other good work. You only allow those things after you have completed X amount of work. This motivates you and it allows you to work less interrupted. The same goes for checking your phone – put it on silent and allow yourself to check it once an hour for five minutes.

Doing this helps to prevent procrastination because your willpower doesn't have to be so strong as to *completely* avoid ever doing that thing. Instead, it just has to be strong enough to hold off for a while.

Want to become the most incredible, unstoppable version of yourself?

I'm not talking about the usual 'self-help' stuff. This goes beyond being a little better with the opposite sex, or being a little more productive.

Want to take on all new challenges, explore new frontiers, grow and transform yourself?

Then the answer is to overcome your fear. Your fear is what is holding you back. Your fear is what is making you less capable and less formidable. And your fear is what is taking away from your happiness and your fulfillment.

It's time we destroyed fear once and for all and unlocked our full potential.

If we want to learn how to really conquer fear, then we can turn to some examples from history. Some of the most fearless, formidable warriors of all were the samurai. So how did they achieve this complete lack of fear?

According to legend, there was a technique that the samurai would practice right before battle in order to eliminate their fear. To do this, they would vividly imagine every possible way that they could be killed. They would imagine being impaled, dismembered and decapitated.

Then they would focus on accepting these possibilities and coming to terms with them. They would become okay with a horrific and brutal death.

The samurai were actually a very morbid and fatalistic bunch. The Bushido code explained that it was an honor to die in battle and that they should *constantly* keep their mind on death.

You'd think this would make them more fearful but paradoxically, it empowered them to be the completely ruthless, fearless warriors that they were. This makes sense: if you fear death, then you will fear life.

If the samurai have accepted the worst thing that could happen to them and if they have come to terms with it, then what reason have they to be afraid?

Now imagine fighting someone who has zero fear of death: who is willing to put themselves at risk, to launch 100% into a movement and not be concerned with the potential outcome. They would be *devastating*.

The good news is that we live in a much less dangerous time and you probably *don't* need to come to terms with your death in quite the same way. But we can take this same notion and we can look at ways to apply it to our own lives.

- First, identify the goal or thing you would like to change. Let's say you want to quit your job and start your own business.

- Next, write down all of the things you are afraid of and all of the things that could go wrong. First, your partner might think you are irresponsible and they might leave you. Second, your new business might fail and you'll be left with debt. Third, your house might get repossessed. Fourth, you might end up vagrant. Fifth, your friends might laugh at you. Sixth, it might all go to plan but you find you hate your new position even more. You get the idea.

- Now score each of those things on how *honestly likely* they are to happen. Would your partner really leave you? It's unlikely unless there are problems in your marriage, to begin with, so we can give that a '2'. Would you end up destitute or would you probably find another job, even if it's a step down from what you were doing before? Give that one a '3'.

- Next: do these things really matter? Score them 1-10. If your friends judge you... who cares?

- Now, you're going to go through that list again and you're going to write down all the ways you could cope with the things that go wrong. These are your contingency plans and the things that you could do to cope. For instance, if you ended up broke you could get benefits, you could dip into your savings, you could ask your parents for help, you could take on a part-time job. If your partner left you, you could fulfill that dream of traveling the world.

- Then go through the list *another* time. This time, write down all the ways you can mitigate the risk so that it is less likely to happen. Worried about getting into debt? Then write a business model that doesn't involve a substantial upfront expense and bootstrap your way to success. Worried about leaving your job? Then start your business in your free time first.

Now you're going to do something else: you're going to think about the worst case scenario if you *don't* follow through with your plan.

That might be that you end up stuck in a job you hate. That one day you'll be 80 years old and you'll look back on your life and feel that you never made anything of it. That your body and your mind atrophied from lack of challenge or experience.

What's worse? I know how I feel!

And focus on what we discussed in that section on stoicism: bad things *will* happen. You can't possibly avoid all bad things happening.

Meanwhile, you are only responsible for your own emotions. You can't make everyone happy all of the time so don't even try. What you should focus on is accepting this reality and then just doing what you need to for your own emotional and psychological well-being in the meantime.

You can't live without taking chances because of someone else your whole life or you will be filled with resentment. And you could die tomorrow, or lose your legs in a car accident. Maybe your partner might run off with another man/woman!

How they react to your decision is up to them. But you can't let that define your actions.

You can't hold onto things just the way they are. You can't prevent bad things from happening. All you can do is live life to its fullest and richest right now. That's why you *have* to take those chances.

The above technique can work when you need to make a big decision or plot the course of your life. But what about that acute fear? That short-term fear?

Here, the exact same process comes into effect. Scared to speak up in public? Then quickly run through that fear-setting technique where you consider the possible outcomes and why they don't *really* matter. You ultimately have two choices: stay quiet and *remain* fearful, or take chances and grow as a person so that you're less scared next time.

Thinking of doing a bungee jump? Then again, run through all the things that could go wrong and how likely/serious they are. Sure, the rope could snap or turn out to be too long, but you know that the likelihood of that happening is somewhere in the region of 0.0001% or less.

Not only that, but it would be over instantly, you'd never know anything about it.

And you can't live your life in fear.

So, jump!

If you have a crippling fear of public speaking, then you get out on stage and you *purposefully* give a rubbish speech. You experience that 'worst case scenario' first hand and you prove to yourself that it really isn't that bad.

In doing this, you can learn to desensitize yourself from the things you would normally find scary and you can become a much more fearless and confident version of yourself.

And this is really the very best way to overcome fear: it's to keep pushing yourself and challenging yourself. Keep subjecting yourself to the very things you find daunting. Fear is a good sign – it's a sign that you're growing – and the more you practice keeping your mind calm and steady in these situations, the more you will find that reaction comes naturally.

And one more thing, remember to breathe! Breathing deeply will activate your rest and digest system – the parasympathetic nervous system – and this will slow your heart rate and subdue your panic response.

Keep your eye on the prize: if you can eventually eliminate fear, you can take on *any* challenge and succeed.

Your health is the source of *all* your power. The way you feel when you wake up first thing in the morning is what will determine how much you can get done that day. Your health impacts directly on your mood and motivation, your ability to complete physically or mentally demanding tasks and even your looks. Then there's the fact that your health will determine how *long* you live and the quality of your life *during* that span.

In other words, your health is the single, most important thing to consider if you want to make life objectively better. And yet it's something that many of us don't give any thought to.

Seriously: most of us will give *far* more focus to our careers, whether or not the house is tidy and what our friends think of us than we will to our physical strength, the condition of our heart or how much body fat we're carrying around.

And it should come as no surprise then that a *huge* proportion of us are *incredibly* unhealthy. Many of us will drive to work every day and then spend *all day* sitting in an office in a hunched position while feeling very stressed. We come home and eat a ready-made meal which is packed with salt and sugar and zero nutrients and then we crash out on the couch before having a fitful and all-too-brief night's sleep.

Then we wonder why we are overweight, unattractive, tired, depressed and prone to illness.

Hmm!

The big problem is that many of us don't know how to go about fixing this problem and becoming healthier. And moreover, many of us think that getting into a healthy place is going to involve a large amount of work and effort – too much for us to attempt.

Maybe you've had a go at a new training program or diet at some point and found that it didn't provide the results you were looking for? Or maybe you gave it a go and then just ran out of energy.

Fixing Your Fitness

The mistake that most people make when trying to improve their health and fitness is that they aim too high. Their objective is often to try and transform their bodies into these athletic specimens that they see on magazine covers when they are currently barely able to make it up the stairs.

This is particularly apparent when running. Lots of people give up on running because they find it *horrible*. And they find it horrible because they push themselves too hard – they run too fast and too far because they want to become top runners or they want to burn thousands of calories.

But the best approach to running is to first simply focus on becoming *better at running*. Better yet, you should learn to *like running*.

To do this, you should go for shorter runs to begin with and you should take them more slowly. Go for a light jog through a scenic area and come home as soon as you stop enjoying it. Do this regularly enough and you'll eventually start to enjoy and look forward to those runs. This is when they can start to transform your fitness and your lifestyle.

Running once or twice a week even just gently like this will help you to train your heart. The difference this can make to your happiness and health should never be underestimated. When you run, you will specifically be strengthening and enlarging the left ventricle. The end result is that your heart will be able to pump more blood around the body with fewer beats. In turn, this means that your crucial 'resting heart rate' metric will slow down. Your heart will beat less as you train, which in turn will result in your sympathetic tone being better. In other words, you will be *less stressed* all of the time and your heart will be far less prone to hypertension.

But running might not be for you. This might be beyond you. Another great type of exercise to start up then is resistance training AKA weightlifting.

Weightlifting can transform your life and this is something that *far* more people should consider.

Many women – and in fact many men as well – will turn away from the idea of weightlifting because they don't want to become overly bulky or muscular. The point that these people are missing, is that it is impossible to 'accidentally' become too bulky or muscular. Arnold Schwarzenegger did not get to his size by accident! Rather, in order to get to that kind of size, you need intensive training and work.

A more moderate training program will simply give you tone, power and greater control over your body. And guess what? Building muscle will help you to lose a lot of weight because simply *having* muscle will increase your metabolism to the point that you'll be burning more calories even as you sleep. Oh, and it also gives you the ideal proportions you want.

A great training program for beginners to try is PPL – Push Pull Legs. That means you train all pushing movements one day, all pulling movements another and then legs on the third day. Again, don't push yourself too hard too fast. Focus on enjoying the training and just using your body in new ways.

You are *not* an athlete and there's no rush here. There's no reason to push yourself beyond what you find enjoyable.

Finally, note that you also need to be more active the rest of the time. Two or three one hour sessions a week will not make up for a sedentary lifestyle. So start to incorporate walking into your routine – this is a fantastic way to burn an extra 2-300 calories a day and that amounts to 1,000 to 1,500 calories a every work week!

Likewise, consider taking up a class, be that martial arts, dance or something else active that will get you into shape. I need to say this, sex can burn lots of calories and help you stay fit and in a positive mindset too, just saying!

The Evolutionary Shadow

If it is so deeply ingrained in us that we must go after the things we want in life, keep taking on new challenges and move out of our comfort zone to become something new… then why is it that so many of us eventually end up in dead-end jobs and feeling rather unfulfilled as a result?

This may come down to something called the evolutionary shadow.

Remember how evolution works? It is all about survival. The person who survives passes on their traits – which presumably are positive traits seeing as they helped them survive. Thus, all our DNA is made up of previous 'winners' and our psychology is optimized to help us live and thrive.

Problem is, evolution doesn't care about us past 30… maybe past 35.

Why? Because once you reach that age, you've already *had* your children most likely (or you're in a situation where you are ready to). You've passed on your surviving genes and you've fulfilled your role. Therefore, it doesn't matter what happens to you after.

And this is seen reflected in the way we live our lives. Once we find a stable career and raise our kids, all the journey, discovery, newness and adventure is gone from our lives. We get into a rut and we start to move backward instead of forward.

The movies reflect this too: it's why there are so few stories about married couples. So few stories about princes that have already *become* kings and now must deal with the day-to-day administration.

And this is why our lives can often feel like they lack meaning. It's because they lack direction.

Actualization *is* apotheosis. Actualization is *growth*. It is becoming the best that we can be.

The quote often used to describe actualization is:

"What a man can be, he must be."

If you are not fulfilling your potential, or moving towards a better version of you… then you are moving backward.

The brain literally comes to life when it has a goal, when we learn new things and when we give it challenge. It becomes more youthful and plastic as it produces more dopamine, more norepinephrine and more BDNF (brain-derived neurotrophic factor). Our memories improve, our attention improves and we become more energetic and positive.

As soon as you stop doing that though, you greatly increase your risk of starting to develop Alzheimer's and other forms of cognitive decline. Your body is always changing and your only choice is whether it moves forward or backward.

In order to get what you want from life, you first need to know what that is. How can you fulfill your potential if you don't know who you are or what makes you happy?

This is why goal setting is such a crucial skill to cultivate and something that everyone should spend more time learning. I have dedicated an entire chapter to hypnotic goal setting but here are some basics. If you don't know what your goals are, then life becomes a little like going on a journey with no destination. Even if you might enjoy the journey, you're still going to risk ending up somewhere you don't want to be and you certainly won't take the most efficient route to get there!

So, it's simple right? You just have to ask yourself what you really want from life and then go and get it. Right?

Unfortunately not. Unfortunately, goal setting is anything *but* easy and is very much a skill in itself. The problem is that not many people realize this and they never think to assess the quality of the goals themselves. They blame their motivation, their circumstances or even other people.

But rarely do they assess whether the fault might lie with the goal itself.

5 GET INTO MINDFULNESS

If there is one ability that you could learn that would make every single aspect of your life better, what would it be? Undoubtedly, it would be the ability to control your emotions and to control the way you think.

This might sound like a surprising claim but the ability to control your emotions and the way you respond to a situation is not only the secret to happiness, but also the secret to being able to get whatever you want from life. Have you ever seen the program on TV called "The Secret" it talks about the law of attraction and the law of Mindfulness, it is brilliant and reinforces this chapter.

Why is controlling your thoughts and emotions important? Because it's our interpretation of events, more than the events themselves, that dictate our happiness, mood and performance. Not only that, but our emotions and the neurotransmitters that control them are what alter our ability to focus, to remember information and to be creative.

The reaction of your body is in response to your belief and your perception not the reality. Chemical reactions are caused by subconscious thoughts that actually make you react the way you do.

If you could gain control of your emotional response then, you could prevent a stressful response and instead stay calm and focussed.

The ability to increase your confidence can actually lead to all kinds of changes in your life that result in you being more productive, more successful... even wealthier.

And it doesn't stop there! Controlling your emotions also means you'll be able to overcome stressful situations and even phobias! Say goodbye to a fear of public speaking... And likewise, controlling your emotions can help you to avoid arguments and shouting matches in your relationship – which will result in a more harmonious and happy home life.

Then there are the ways that your emotion can make you more powerful and more efficient. Did you know for instance, that you can increase muscle fiber recruitment and potentially tap into a superhuman strength by getting into the right mood? Did you know that the correct combination of neurochemistry can give you perfect recall?

So what exactly is mindfulness?

Essentially, mindfulness is a form of self-hypnosis that has been adopted many hypnotists use it as a way to help their clients outside of an actual hypnotic session. Think of mindfulness as a hybrid between meditation and hypnosis.

Mindfulness essentially gives us a tool that we can use to not only calm our thoughts and escape the stressors of the day but *also* reflect on the contents of our mind in the interests of self-improvement.

The idea behind mindfulness then is not to try and empty your thoughts but instead to simply step back from them and 'observe' them like a detached third party. This way, you are not letting your thoughts affect you and make you stressed but you also are not going to struggle with not being 'allowed' to think anything. People experience that holistic out of body view of themselves. In the British Army we used to call it "Helicopter Vision"

Meanwhile, using this technique will also allow you to become more aware of your own thoughts and thereby able to edit any thoughts that are leading you into trouble. For instance, if you constantly find yourself thinking about the ways that you could hurt yourself, you might notice that this is a bad habit and then attempt to fix that.

This is what mindfulness refers to in most cases but it has also been appropriated to mean a lot more. If mindfulness means being more aware of your thoughts, then it can also be applied outside of meditation and to the way you go about your day. In this case, mindfulness simply means being mindful of what you're focussing on and what you're thinking at any given point. This is useful because very often you'll find that your mind isn't perhaps where it should be.

For example, if you are walking through a beautiful scenic woodland but you are thinking about work, then as far as your body is concerned you may as well *be* at work. In this case, mindfulness can be used simply to make yourself more aware of where you are and to actually focus on what's around you. That means feeling the breeze on your skin, looking at the beautiful flowers and smelling the fresh air. When you do all that, you will benefit much more from the experience.

Likewise, you can use mindfulness to direct your attention to all manner of other things. For example, your physical sensations. Often we are not aware of just how we're sitting, how we're standing or how we're feeling.

Take a moment right now to reflect on this. How comfortable are you at the moment? Does any part of your body hurt? If you're sitting down, then where is most pressure on you? Can you feel your clothes against your body? A watch maybe? How warm are you? Are you leaning more to one side?

This kind of mindfulness can be useful if you want to try and fix your posture but also if you want to improve your abilities in sports or just move more efficiently.

Being more mindful of the way you speak can meanwhile help you to speak more eloquently, to stop using derogatory words, to stop swearing, or to change the whole way that people perceive you. For example, if you want to sound more intelligent, then you can simply try using bigger words or speaking a little more slowly.

You can also use mindfulness to be happier in everyday life. Simply try to stop letting negative emotions affect you by identifying them as temporary and destructive. You can simply 'notice' that you're getting angry and acknowledge that your thoughts will be tainted by that. With practice, this can make you a much calmer and much happier person.

Practicing mindfulness both as a form of self-hypnosis *and* during the day can therefore help you to improve your ability to control your thoughts and thereby to decide how you want to improve yourself and what you want to focus on.

Generally, most mindfulness self-hypnosis will take very similar steps and you can go through the steps without necessarily needing to be talked through it. And in fact, if you *can* perform your self-hypnosis without guidance, then you should find that you're actually more effective at it because you won't be continuously interrupted by someone's voice.

Let's go over what the steps will *generally* be for a mindfulness session...

Step 1: Breathing

The first thing to do is to start breathing. You can do this using something called 'equal breathing' from yoga. Here, you breathe in through the nose and out through the mouth. As you do, you hold each inhalation and exhalation for 3 seconds (hence the 'equal' bit). These long draws in and long exhalations will allow you to completely fill the lungs with fresh oxygen and expel all the CO_2.

But you can use any kind of breathing so long as it is slow, deliberate and full. The guidance they give on the Headspace App, for instance, is simply to 'breathe loud enough so that the person next to you would be able to hear'.

Why the breathing? Essentially, breathing slowly is the best way to indicate to the body that the coast is clear and you're safe. We breathe quickly when we're stressed to get more oxygen around our bodies and we can breathe more slowly when we are relaxed. Thus, breathing deeply and slowly will help us to exit the 'fight or flight' state and instead enter the 'rest and digest' state. This should fix our heart rate variance, reduce cortisol and get us ready to enter a relaxed state.

Step 2: Senses

Next, you are often told to focus on your physical senses. This means noticing the smells, sounds and even the temperature around the room. Your eyes will normally be closed, so sight is ruled out of this one.

The objective here is not to 'look' for sounds or strain to hear them. Instead, just notice the sounds that you don't normally. You might find that you can hear creaking in the house, maybe you can hear the neighbors, maybe you can hear the rain outside or the wind. There are probably far off birds and/or traffic.

This is always a fantastic example of just how little we normally pay attention to and how much richer our experience becomes when we practice mindfulness. It's also a great way to get into that habit and to start relaxing the body even more.

Step 3: Body Scan

Body scan is sometimes described as being its own thing but it can be used as part of any meditation session. The idea here is simply to become more aware of your own body as we described earlier but to do this by systematically starting at the top of the head and then moving gradually through to the toes, noticing how you feel at each stage.

If you want to use this process to get to sleep, then it can be a great tool for that purpose too. The best way to do this though is to try completely relaxing the muscles by first tensing and then releasing each part of your body as you move through it. What you'll find is that you carry large amounts of tension everywhere from your face muscles, to your neck, to your arms and legs. Once you recognize this and let it go, you'll feel far more relaxed and eventually this can enable you to fall into a deep and restful sleep.

For now, though, we're just scanning the body and using this as a way to become more mindful of ourselves and to begin the process of introspection and self-directed attention.

Step 4: Focus on Breathing

After noticing each part of the body, return to the chest and pay particular attention to the way it rises and falls. As you do this, you can also take this opportunity to fix your breathing.

Chances are, that when you first notice your own breathing, you'll find that you are breathing in so that your chest expands first. But in fact, it should be your abdomen that moves first and this should then be *followed* by your chest. Correct breathing (called abdominal breathing) should start by allowing the stomach to relax and protrude and then filling the lungs.

This is effective because the process opens up space in your abdominal cavity. This then allows the lungs to expand *into* that space, which is then followed by them expanding upwards through your chest as well.

This type of breathing allows you to take in more oxygen and to trigger even more relaxation hormones. Most of us don't use this kind of breathing though because we have hunched postures which fold our stomach and prevent us from being able to breathe from there. The result is that we end up breathing with much shallower and faster breaths, which actually increases stress and cortisol.

But don't worry about that if you don't want to. For now, just notice your own breath and take this opportunity to count your breaths as they come in and out. This is the part that is going to work a little like transcendental hypnosis by quietening down a lot of the activity throughout the brain.

Step 5: Let Your Mind Wander

Once you've done this for a little while and you're feeling particularly still, it's time to just let go of your mind and let it do whatever it wants. Now your aim is not to try and control or silence your thoughts. Instead, you simply let your mind wander naturally – or stay completely still if it wants to.

The description that is often used is that you're 'watching thoughts go by like clouds'. Headspace describes your thoughts in these cases as being more like cars on the road. It emphasizes the importance of watching the 'cars' go past but not running out into the road to chase the traffic. This is all about detached observation.

After you have done this for a while, you can simply allow your mind to gradually return to normal and gently open your eyes.

If you really want help jump-starting your progress, consider 'priming' yourself. Priming is a term used in psychology that simply refers to preparing the brain in a certain way. Sometimes that means influencing the answers we give to questions by showing certain stimulus. But in other cases, it means changing our emotions. In this case, it pays to do something calming but that nevertheless requires focus just before you try meditating. So for example, you might try relaxing in a beautiful but novel location. Novel scenery increase neurotransmitters and hormones associated with focus, while being in natural environments has been shown to make us more relaxed and to encourage slower brainwaves.

Most people believe that we think in 'thoughts'. That is to say that we have an inner monologue that works like the thought boxes in comic books. More recent research though suggests that we can think in lots of modalities: sometimes we visualize, sometimes we imagine our bodies doing something and almost 'feel' what we're thinking and sometimes we just 'know'. This latter example is called 'unsymbolized thought'.

And in fact, thinking with our bodies and our senses might just be what enabled us to develop thought in the first place…

Briefly, embodied cognition is the idea that all our thoughts eventually relate back to physical experience.

When someone says something to you, or when you think something, your brain interprets this in such a way that gives it meaning. You don't inherently understand language, which means the brain must be 'translating' it into some kind of pure meaning.

Psychologists once believed that the brain had a language of its own that they called 'mentalese'. More recently though, more and more experts adopted the belief that we understand things by visualizing them. When someone says tells you a story, you understand the story because your brain visualizes it happening to you.

When someone tells you they walked through the snow, you visualize the color white, you imagine the cool air on your skin and you almost hear the sound of the crunching snow underfoot. When we think 'higher level' thoughts, we understand them only because we can relate them back to physical experiences via abstraction. Maths, after all, is fundamentally based on counting...

This is also consistent with the idea that areas of our brain light up during visualization just as though we were really engaging in the action. If you imagine swinging a golf club, then neurons relating to that movement will fire in your brain.

And as far as your brain and body is concerned, that might as well be happening!

So it makes a lot of sense to combine visualization with your self-hypnosis training and with your restructuring. Don't believe that visualization can 'trick' your brain into thinking something is happening and thereby alter your emotional state? Then just try relieving your most upsetting moments, or imagining scenes from a very sad movie. You'll start to feel incredibly sad in no time...

One way to use this power of visualization that is well understood, is to go to a 'happy place' during self-hypnosis. If you cannot use self-hypnosis in a calm and beautiful environment, then at least you can simulate it in your mind's eye by imagining you're on a beautiful beach, in a log cabin in the mountains, or in a large field getting plenty of sun.

But you can also use visualization in order to alter your emotional state in other ways.

For example, if you're struggling to focus on your work, then you might utilize visualization to create a little eustress to motivate you. To do this, you simply need to remember *why* you're doing the work and why it's important to you. Let's say that you're working towards a presentation for a meeting: visualize just how great it would feel to conquer that presentation and knock it out the part. Then visualize what doing that repeatedly could one day lead to: a better career and a better salary for instance.

Now visualize the opposite: imagine it going wrong and remember why it matters.

You can do the same thing with almost anything you're struggling to focus on. By linking what you're doing back to the emotional hook and the reason you're doing it, you can much more effectively find the determination and drive you need to complete it. Keep your goals in mind and you'll be much more motivated every day to get out of bed and start working out, or to work on your personal project, or to put in your very best performance at work.

This is one reason we're often told to visualize ourselves obtaining our goals. When you visualize yourself obtaining a goal, you produce neurotransmitters and hormones *as though* you had achieved that goal. As far as your brain is concerned, that has already happened. This then makes you much more likely to perform well when you actually attempt that thing.

Likewise though, when we *unintentionally* visualize ourselves falling, or stuttering up on stage, this actually causes us to produce more fight or flight hormones which in turn makes us nervous and makes us much more likely to actually do those things.

So don't just restructure your thoughts, try to picture things going well – and with the backing of your cognitive restructuring you should know that this is actually what's more *likely* to happen.

In general, removing anxiety and increasing our confidence is a very important tool and the more you can recognize the power of simply believing in your own ability, the more things will start to go your way.

Another tool you can use then is to completely remove social anxiety using hypothesis testing. Most of us have *some* social anxiety even if we're generally confident and by removing this, we can become much more successful.

Let's start by asking why confidence matters in the first place. The simple answer is that when you're confident, others think they should *also* be confident in you. This sends the evolutionary signal that you must be higher in the pecking order than them – it makes the opposite sex think that you must be a good catch and it makes the same sex think that you must be an important and influential figure.

But when we stutter and stammer, it suggests that we aren't confident in either the content of what we're saying, or our own importance. Either way, this then makes people less likely to believe us and it makes them think that if we're shy of them, they must be superior to us. The hierarchy has now established us in a much weaker position. It doesn't mean they'll be cruel, it simply means that we're not in a position of power and influence.

Using hypothesis testing, it's possible to go one step further and to completely transform the way that people think of you and the way you interact with others.

To do this, you're simply going to remove the anxiety you previously had when speaking to people by testing the outcome of it going wrong. So find a shop that you don't often shop in and then go up to the counter to order something. When you do, do it using a funny voice, say something purposefully awkward, or stand in silence for a moment. It will be awkward and painful and it will trigger your fight or flight response. But breathe and try not to get too anxious. What you'll learn is that nothing bad comes of this experiment and the transaction is completed as normal.

That was the worst case scenario and nothing bad happened! Do this a bit more and over time, the re-association will also kick in and you'll learn that there's really nothing to be afraid of. Eventually things like interviews, dates and other social scenarios will be far less scary and will trigger much less of a stress response. The result? You'll seem so confident and at ease, that your charisma and influence will increase drastically.

But even without this step, simply practicing mindfulness and learning to distance yourself from your thoughts will help you to become calmer and more confident. And it will also help you to detach from negative emotions and thereby increase your self-value. There are even types of self-hypnosis that involve meditating about the things you love about yourself.

However, you achieve it, increasing your self-worth and confidence can eventually start to make all kinds of things happen in your life. This is called 'the law of attraction' and it simply means that when you believe yourself to be one way, you *become* that way.

So when you think of yourself as a highly successful high flyer who will no doubt be rich one day, that's how others will perceive you and that's how you'll act. You'll present yourself as someone more confident, you'll take on jobs with more responsibility and you'll even dress the part. And when others think of you that way and you start taking more opportunities for promotions etc., then you'll start to actually climb the ladder.

6 INCREASE YOUR FOCUS

In our lives today, we are busier than ever before. We think technology has streamlined many tasks, but instead, we are given more tools that give us more and more to do with less time to do it. We are stressed and overwhelmed. The phrase "time management" has become taboo, since it implies there are different ways to cram even more into our already overflowing lives.

We have been led to believe that if we don't multitask every minute of our day we will not be productive. This can't be further from the truth. Successful people have long realized that focus is the key to being productive.

> Most of what we say and do is not essential. If you can eliminate it, you'll have more time, and more tranquility. Ask yourself at every moment, 'Is this necessary?' ~Marcus Aurelius

Increasing your focus means you should get up each day, looking forward to what you can achieve. Being focused means you are making progress towards what is most important to you. You will feel a greater sense of productivity and fulfillment.

Being focused on one thing for a certain period of time allows you to do a better quality of work, more work gets done quicker, and your creative ideas flow easier. Being focused on one task at a time is less stressful on your mind. And being less stressed allows you be happier.

It's difficult for people to remain focused on one task for a variety of reasons. For one, we live in a world where we are constantly bombarded with TV, radio, cell phones, Internet social media, as well as a much larger population that lives closer together than ever before.

It's difficult to get away from all these distractions completely. One way is to go to a room where you can shut your door and turn off your phone and email notifications.

- When you focus on a single task, avoiding distractions, your brain becomes focused on that task alone. This lets you complete that task much more quickly than if you are trying to complete two or more tasks at once. For instance, let's say you need to write a blog post, do your bookkeeping for the week and research information for an upcoming speech. The best thing to do is to set aside all but one task. So, for this example, you want to give all your attention writing your blog post. That means turning off the TV, cell phones, social media pings, closing your door and putting all your attention on writing.

- By giving all your attention to the task without distraction, you can get it done much more quickly and with fewer mistakes. Your work will be higher quality as well. Another benefit to being focused is that your creativity will kick in too. You'll come up with new ideas associated with the task at hand.

This is great if you are someone who creates in some way. This includes traditional creative types like artists, writers, photographers, designers and musicians, as well as people who create products or services, teachers, researchers, stay-at-home parents, executives, bloggers, and anyone who needs ideas. This means just about everyone can benefit.

- Being constantly connected to others and having many distractions that take away your focus can affect your stress levels as well as your productivity. When you aren't focused, you don't get as much done as you could if you were truly focused on the task you're doing.

- Focusing on one thing for a certain period helps you think better. Having your mind scattered over several tasks at once keeps you from thinking about what you are actually doing. You only have time to complete a task quickly before you must move on to the next one. All the while you are trying to remember everything that has to be done. When you focus, you are able to think about only one thing for that period.

- Focusing allows your subconscious to do the work. Think about when you learned to ride a bike or drive a car. It was difficult in the beginning, but when you began focusing on what you were doing, your subconscious took over and helped you learn. The same is true in your everyday tasks. Once you begin focusing solely on one task, your subconscious helps you do them quicker and easier.

It's important to focus on one task at a time to become more productive, do better quality work and be less stressed. Focusing can help you be more creative and have more happiness.

Multitasking is overrated

If you're like many people, you spend most days multitasking. You're probably so used to multitasking that you don't even realize when you're doing it. After all, it's a skill many employers look for in their employees. Many people believe multitasking saves them time. There are many reasons why multitasking is bad. It's better to focus instead though. Focusing lets you concentrate on one task or thought at a time, helping you create a better result for each task.

Many people like to multitask because they become bored working on one task at a time.

Why is multitasking bad?

You have to switch from task to task. This takes time for your mind to change into the right mindset for the new task. You have to take the time to remember where you left off.

1. Multitasking leads to attention and memory loss. According to a study by Harvard Professor Clifford Nass, in findings published in the Proceedings of the National Academy of Science, people who use online social media and other forms of electronic communications have trouble focusing their attention and have lower scores on memory tests.

2. Cognitive performance is diminished. A recent study by Zheng Wang, a professor at Ohio State University, showed that multitasking caused students to feel more productive, but showed they were actually reducing their cognitive skills abilities such as studying.

3. Multitaskers lose productivity. Switching between tasks is counter-productive. You lose time and concentration every time you switch to a different task.

4. Multitaskers are less likely to finish one quality project. They may finish all their tasks for the day, but they will most likely be sub-par than if they had focused solely on one to completion.

Multitasking makes it difficult to focus entirely on each task you are doing. You are thinking about emails you have to respond to when writing a report and the phone calls you need to return even while you are thinking about the next task on your to-do list. This type of working environment doesn't do anything but will only add stress to your life. Instead of multitasking among several tasks, you should prioritize your tasks and break them up into workable time chunks.

Having an end goal in mind while working on the tasks to achieve it can frustrate you because you target goal might be too big or difficult. Your results won't be quick, and it may seem like you aren't getting any closer to the end. Instead of working toward the ultimate end goal, break it down into smaller, more achievable goals you can reach within a few days. Then cross each smaller goal off your list as you achieve it.

Work within your body's most comfortable time. Maybe you work best early in the morning before sunrise. Or late at night. Work when you are most productive. For example, many authors get up early to do their writing, while artists often do their best work late at night.

Have you ever eaten a big meal for lunch when working only to feel lethargic and weighed down all afternoon? Eating a heavy meal slows you down and makes you sleepy. If you need or want to, you can go on a small juice fast on a regular basis. It will keep you alert and help keep your body in good physical condition.

Exercise your mind and body every day. Do crossword puzzles. Engage in lively discussions. Build something that's creative. A simple 30 minute walk every day is all you need to keep your body healthy.

You may need to push yourself some when you're feeling lazy. If you are hitting a mental roadblock, though, take some time away from the task. Do something else until you can regain your focus on the original task. Learning to improve your focus will take time but it is worth it. Begin by implementing one or two of these tips into your day to begin changing how well you can become focused.

You'd be surprised by how many people lose track of where their time goes. They might think they are focused on a single task, but are they really? One way to find out is to keep track of how you spend your time for a week. You might find out you've been wasting time on little things like checking Facebook once an hour. Use my free Time Management Calculator to see where your time is going https://www.hypnoticsuccesshabits.com/free-time-calculator

Here are my strategies for improving your focus and increasing your productivity:

1. Track your time. Analyze the results after a week. Tweak and get rid of time wasters. Yes, use the free calculator.

2. Plan your week. At the end of your week, find a quiet spot to plan out your week's tasks. Write down key projects and the tasks associated with them. Don't forget to add in family activities that you participate in as well. You can use my Hypnotic Goals Planner to do this. I have a 390-page printed journal for your use available on Amazon or you can download the eBook version to jot down your goals and tasks.

3. Prioritize your list. Break down your tasks from most important to least important. Use a calendar to mark out blocks of uninterrupted time (anywhere from 15 to 60 minutes) to work on each one.

4. Eliminate what isn't essential. Outsource what you can for things you need to do but which aren't your strengths. This could be anything from mowing your lawn to hiring a virtual assistant to take care of your social media for the week.

5. Set your goals. Break down big or long-term goals into smaller, weekly or daily goals to make them easier to focus on.

6. Set aside a specific amount of time each day for checking/answering email and social media. It could be the first 30-minute task of the day, the last 30 minutes of your workday, or maybe the 15 minutes before your lunch break. Only do it once a day though. Don't be stopping in the middle of a task to check your email. The same goes for social media channels as well.

7. Do away with multitasking. It takes a while to learn how to focus on one project at a time, but stick with it and it will become a habit. Finish one project/task before moving on to the next one. Become laser-focused on one task at a time. This can really increase your productivity.

8. Make a distraction to-do list. The Internet has made it easy for us to become quickly distracted. As soon as we want to look something up, we hop on the Internet to do a search. "I wonder what's happening on Facebook." "What was the name of the actor in that movie?" "How long will it take me to drive to the zoo tomorrow?" Anytime we get distracted like this it takes about 25 minutes to get back to the original task. So instead, next time you want to look up something or an idea pops in your head, jot it down on a piece of paper (or, even better, use Evernote).

9. Learn to say NO. If you already have full day's task list, don't feel like you have to take on another project for someone else.

10. Create an environment that works for you. Do you need a quiet space, free from people, phones and television noise? Set up your office so it works for you. Decorate it in soothing colors, inspiring artwork and a comfortable chair. If you work best in a neat and clean area, make sure you put away or file papers and magazines. Get rid of clutter. If you focus better while listening to music or some kind of ambient noise, be sure to have a way to make that happen.

11. Take a break when needed. Short breaks help break up boredom and burnout when you're working on a big project. Get up and walk around the room. Do some yoga stretches.

12. Break up or Chunk it. Break your tasks down into smaller more manageable chunks of time with short breaks in between. For example, work on a task in 15-minute chunks. For example, let's say you're writing an eBook. Don't try to do the whole thing at once. Break it down. Take 15 minutes to write out your outline. Take a short break. Then 15 minutes to research the first chapter. And so on.

13. Use an app on your phone to boost your productivity and concentration. Apps like Evernote can keep you organized and keep track of distractions. You can download an app like Brainwave to your iPhone. In this app, you can choose settings like Concentration Boost and Problem Solving, Brainstorming, or Memory Boost and Creative Thinking. There are other apps that help you stay focused and productive as well.

The strategies for becoming more focused are endless. Make lists. Remove distractions. Set up your ideal environment. You need to find what works best for your style of working.

You probably already know how hard it is to focus on something. Focus issues are often the result of different things like boredom, lack of interest or even fatigue. Concentration can often be attributed to how motivated and interested we are in the task.

Supplements can help you when you are having focus issues. Vitamins like the B complex group, Biotin or vitamin H and lecithin all help improve your memory.

Eating the right foods can help you better focus as well since you will be getting the supplements from the foods to help with brain health. Foods like lean meat, beans, oranges, peanut butter and oysters.

Consult with your physician if you find you can't focus on any one thing for any length of time. Lack of focus can be a symptom of several different conditions, including depression. Get a thorough checkup to rule out any physical causes of your lack of focus issues.

When working on projects on your computer and online, make sure you only have tabs open that are relevant to what you are doing. This keeps you from getting distracted by all that fun information floating around the Internet.

Make your tasks routine. Set up a routine for tasks that you do every day. For example, check your email and social media at the same time every day. Just like you probably have a routine when you wake up, you should also have a routine when working.

Separate your day into a time for creating, time for work and communication, and time for yourself. Split the day up in whatever way works best for you.

Dealing with focus issues causes your productivity to drop. By learning how to take care of your focus issues through your diet, exercise and routines, you can be more productive.

You can increase your productivity and accomplish more in

less time by using a technique called applied focus. Applied focus can help you avoid the little distractions that can derail your efforts at productivity.

Applied focus is a strategy that helps you multiply your productivity. Each session is 45 minutes long, with a 15-minute shift in focus. Or you can do 90 minutes followed by 30-minute shift in focus. In other words, you stop focusing intentionally on your task and do something completely different in the shift focus period. During the focused session, though, you don't allow anything to distract you (except a dire emergency). Phone calls are out, email is off, texting and Facebook are off limits.

Here are some guidelines (be sure to adjust them as necessary to fit your individual situation):

1. Open only one browser or application window at a time. So if you're writing a blog post, only your word processor or text pad is open.

2. Keep your sessions timed. Don't go past your 45 or 90-minute session, no matter how focused you are. You need the break.

3. Get away from your task. Get up from your desk, walk around, get a drink or snack. Give your mind a break.

4. Be prepared ahead of time. Do your research during a different applied focus session then from the writing

session. That way you're able to concentrate on the writing alone.

5. Have a session set up for email, telephone and social media time.

Applied focus sessions can increase your productivity but it will take some getting used to. Start slowly by scheduling one or two sessions a day. Once you become used to the routine, you will notice an improvement in your concentration and productivity.

What's next?

Learning how to focus on one task at a time takes time and commitment. In our busy lives we are pulled in many directions at one time. It's best to begin your journey on a more focused life gradually. Focus is such an important part of how productive you are. If you can focus on one task for a set amount of time you will be more productive in a shorter amount of time than you have been. Putting aside your tendency to multitask will improve your productivity as well, since you will be able to finish one task before you move on.

Removing distractions can help you focus as well. Create an environment that you feel comfortable in, and that fits with how you work. If you're a morning person, then focus on your work tasks, and vice versa for night owls.

Eat healthy and nutritious foods to keep your brain strong and able to concentrate. Exercise daily, use self-hypnosis daily and take time to enjoy nature and your family.

7 GETTING A SMARTER BRAIN

If you could increase your brain power, then theoretically you could accomplish almost anything. While having a healthy and strong body is highly important as well, most of us would probably agree that our activities are more reliant on our cognitive abilities rather than our physical ones.

Much of our success comes down to our ability to interact with others, which of course is very much dependent on our mind, intelligence and our brain power. Whether you're giving a presentation and choosing the best words to communicate your message, or whether you're in an interview or date setting and trying to find the wittiest or funniest response to a question quickly.

Problems at home tend to involve finances, social situations or legal issues – there are very few problems we can solve with our fists. In our spare time, we tend to pursue more intellectual activities too. Perhaps we play video games (reacting to enemies and solving puzzles), or maybe we sit and read.

And even when an activity seems 'physical' on the surface, it is in fact very often just as much cognitive. Take sports for example, which require you to be aware of the positions of your team members and opponents and to use your body efficiently and accurately through space. Or how about doing 'physical labor' such as house repairs – which almost always involves some measure of amateur engineering.

So, if you were smarter then, or if you just had greater command over your mental faculties, you'd be able to:

- Concentrate longer on tasks and get more work done
    - Thereby progressing further in your chosen career and earning more money
    - Thereby giving yourself more free time at the end of each day and giving you fewer things to stress about.
- Come up with unique ideas and novel solutions
    - Thereby potentially making yourself rich, or changing the world in a positive way
    - Thereby solving problems that you face in your daily life
- Improve your physical and sporting ability
- Impress anyone in a conversation
- Become better at any given task, from plumbing to computer games
- Become more self-sufficient and reliant

And even beyond the practical and tangible benefits of boosting your brain power, you'd be able to benefit from simply having a greater appreciation for the world around you. A better understanding of how things work. An enhanced capacity for learning and more incentive to do so…

Perhaps you could improve your understanding and appreciation of the very nature of life and the universe…

It's no mean feat imagining what would be possible with greater brain power – if you yourself were greater. And so perhaps the best place for us to look to is fiction. What if we consider a fictional example of someone who is suddenly bestowed with incredible mental capacity?

And the best recent example of this probably comes from the 2011 film Limitless. In that film, the protagonist Eddie Mora is given a smart drug – a supplement called NZT. This tablet is an experimental drug that has the ability to help anyone to use '100%' of their brains. (Of course, this is a load of nonsense - we already use 100% of our brains! But we'll allow the writers the poetic license.)

When Eddie takes the NZT, he is instantly transformed. He goes from being a slob and a struggling writer, to cleaning up his apartment and his appearance and completing his manuscript – which of course goes on to become a best-seller. He then works out the stock market and begins day trading, becoming rich from his home. He talks several women into bed before winning back his ex with impress displays of intelligence, such as his new ability to speak several languages. He moves into a stunning, luxury apartment and attracts the attention of an investment firm. Eventually, he uses the power and influence he accrues there to run for political office.

All this, because he was able to take control of his brain. Because he was able to see patterns that others missed. Because he 'knew exactly what he had to do'. And because he gained sharper intuition and better cognitive skills.

Now, of course, this is a fiction and in reality, no such pill exists. Neither can we say with certainty that you would see such a huge impact on your life if you were to increase your brain power alone.

But it's certainly a plausible idea that your life might change that much.

And what is very exciting is that there really are ways that you can boost your intelligence – albeit to a slightly lesser degree. There really are ways you can bring about tangible, measurable improvements in your life by focussing on ways to increase your IQ and your focus.

Before we move on, I want to address just one more topic: the power of working FAST and removing the multitasking mentality.

If you have greater concentration and if you can think more quickly, then you can work faster. This is something I've been training both my students and private hypnosis clients and it's something that I genuinely believe helped me to perform very well indeed throughout my Military; Police and Hypnosis career.

During my Masters Degree program, I was also a full-time Police Officer but my ability to work fast is what allowed me to effectively complete more work than all my peers and to maintain great grades with a limited amount of time. In exams, I'd write twice as much as most people and when coupled with a realization of what examiners were looking for (most will mark papers very much by referring to a checklist of things you need to complete) that meant that I could get better grades than perhaps I could have otherwise.

I have learnt to write faster and faster. I have bought myself enough time to start doing other things in the second half of my day – things like creating marketing software like marketing ninja Text and writing articles and blog posts.

Let's start out by looking at the neuroscience of intelligence and precisely how you can go about increasing it from a theoretical standpoint.

So, welcome to your brain. Here, you have a massive interconnected web of neurons which we collectively refer to as your 'connectome'. Think of this like the world's largest mind map, except that it is made from billions of connections.

Each of these neurons represents an experience, an action, a memory or a 'qualia'.

So, for instance, you have your visual cortex (V1) which contains all the neurons responsible for your sight. If you were to open up the back of your skull and stimulate those neurons individually using an electrode (this has actually been tested by the way), then you would see points of light appear in your vision corresponding to the specific neuron!

Likewise, if you were to stimulate neurons in the motor cortex, then this would cause your arm or leg to move, or it might make you feel a sensation in your ear.

Other neurons have different jobs. For instance, there are those that have the role of storing memories. These light up when we recall things that happened to us in the past. Others might make us feel happy or sad. Others might represent aspects of our personality, or our ideas.

These are grouped into clusters in the brain or brain regions, which is why brain damage can end up knocking out very specific abilities or altering our personalities.

And at any given time, multiple brain areas will be active, representing the way in which your brain is being used. So you might have activity in your visual cortex because you are processing the things around you, but you might also have activity in your hippocampus relating to memories associated with the things you're seeing and you might have activity in your prefrontal cortex as you make plans as to what you are about to do.

The neurons are connected via long tales and branches called axons and dendrites. They don't actually come into physical contact with one another, but rather they come very close to touching and leave just a very slight gap called the synapse. When one neuron fires, it causes all of the surrounding neurons to become more excited. And when neurons pass a certain excitement 'threshold', then they fire too.

So, in other words, you might see a duck and this might register as a representation of a duck in your mind's eye. That causes a certain pattern of neurons to fire and those 'action potentials' (the technical term for these electrical charges) will then travel down the axons to related concepts that are 'connected'. These include the likes of memories you might have about ducks, opinions about ducks, duck facts, Donald Duck etc.

But only when enough activity surrounds your 'Donald Duck' cluster of neurons will those actually light up and only then will you experience a memory or a thought of the character.

Neurons can become excited but they really only have two states: on or off. What's less binary though, is the signal that they send and receive. And this is where neurotransmitters come in.

Neurotransmitters are chemicals that exist in the brain that effectively add color and nuance to the communications happening across our brain. These act like hormones in that they are able to change our mood and change the way we feel about something. The difference is that they have a much shorter lifespan and that they act on the brain specifically.

Among other things, neurotransmitters make neurons surrounding them more or less likely to fire and will thereby put the brain in an overall more excited or more inhibited state. At the same time though, they can also increase the likelihood of new connections forming and they can increase the apparent 'importance' of certain activity, thereby directing your attention.

An example is dopamine. Dopamine is an excitatory neurotransmitter, which means that it makes us more aroused and more awake and it increases the chances of neurons firing. When dopamine is released in a part of the brain, which causes us to become more focussed on whatever is happening right there because it tells us that thing is important and worthy of our attention. At the same time, dopamine increases our likelihood of remembering that event because it makes connections in the brain more likely to form. Finally, dopamine makes us more likely to remember things that happened and more likely to stay motivated. Dopamine is often described as the 'reward neurotransmitter' but it would be more accurate to say that it is released in anticipation of reward.

Other neurotransmitters include the likes of serotonin (the 'feel good hormone') of cortisol (the 'stress hormone') and of oxytocin (the 'love' hormone). All these change the way we subjectively experience the world and they have an impact on the nature of the physical change that occurs within the brain.

An area that has been extensively studied by psychologists and neuroscientists in recent years is a subject called 'brain plasticity' or 'neuroplasticity'. This refers to the brain's innate ability to change shape in response to stimulation and activity.

So previously, we believed that the brain was a set shape once we reached adulthood and that it wouldn't change further. What we now know, however, is that the brain continues to grow and adapt as we get older and that it is constantly forming new connections and even birthing new neurons.

In studies, it has been shown that repeatedly engaging in a specific activity will cause the corresponding brain area to change shape. For instance, if you learn to play the cello, then the areas in your motor cortex that are responsible for the sensation and dexterity in your fingertips will get larger and more complex. Likewise, if you play computer games repeatedly, then the brain areas that are responsible for your ability to make out small details on the horizon will improve. Taxi drivers have physically heavier brains than any other professionals, because they change shape in order to accommodate all the new routes and destinations that they commit to memory.

There is a simple rhyme you can remember to understand the way that plasticity works and that is:

"Neurons that fire together, wire together"

In other words, if you continuously repeat the same action over and over again, then eventually the corresponding neurons will wire so that you have committed that sequence of movements to memory.

If you eat a lemon every time you see a certain picture, then you will eventually associate the picture and the lemon so that seeing the picture causes you to get a bitter taste in your mouth. The corresponding neurons fired at the same time so often, that they now have a connection and now activity in one neuron will increase the chances of the other firing.

What's more, is that repeating this connection will reinforce it over time. This occurs via a process called myelination which basically means that the axons are being insulated to protect them against damage and to help the signal to travel more quickly and more efficiently from one neuron to the next.

This is how we rote learn new subjects and it's why someone who has serious memory loss can sometimes still perform tasks like playing complex piano concertos. They simply repeated the movements so many times that they became highly myelinated and protected.

That's a lot of information to take on board and you might be wondering what it's all for. Well, rest assured that this information is important and we have tackled it for a reason. That's because knowing the way your brain works is what is going to allow you to increase your IQ through training, diet and more.

The first 'strategy' and one I don't necessarily and fully endorse but feel you should at least be aware of is to use nootropics. Nootropics are 'smart drugs' which in turn describe both supplements and medications. Generally, anything that can enhance your mental performance in any given capacity can be considered a nootropic. That means that technically something like caffeine could be considered a nootropic because it makes us more focussed, because it prevents us from needing to sleep and because it helps us to memorize things. Always consult your Doctor and do more research than I am offering here. In my study of hypnosis and while writing this book I uncovered this subject and strategy and it may work for you, make your own choices of course.

Most people who use nootropics don't pick just one of these supplements either but rather use a selection of them in conjunction in order to get the precise results they're looking for. Many will work well in conjunction – for instance, if you use piracetam then it is often recommended that you also take a form of choline, seeing as the brain uses choline in order to formulate acetylcholine.

But should you learn more? Do Nootropics work like the film Limitless? If you can take some supplements like these and become smarter, more focussed, more productive and all that… well, then the question is why wouldn't you? Of course, as with all these things, the reality is not quite so simple as the pitch.

Remember that web of neurons in the brain? Well, creativity comes from our ability to explore those different nodes (neurons) and to find novel connections. Creativity really is simply the ability to recombine existent information in interesting ways. You take two ideas or two concepts and you combine them, and then you have a new, novel concept.

But if you increase your dopamine, you increase your focus on one specific brain area. You become more intensely focussed on one concept or one collection of ideas and in doing so, you lose that ability to make novel connections and to come up with new ideas.

A healthy brain is not a brain that feels wired or highly focussed – it is simply one that feels like it normally does but… better. You should have the ability to switch between different brain states and different 'modes' at will.

You also need to consider the risk of tolerance and adaptation. This is the risk that your brain can adapt to the change in chemical balance and thereby become dependent on nootropics in order to function normally. A good example is caffeine. When you drink caffeine, you reduce the action of a substance called adenosine. This happens because caffeine molecules are very similar in size and shape to adenosine molecules. As such, they can end up getting trapped inside the same receptors and thereby preventing adenosine from being effective.

Adenosine is a by-product that is produced when our cells create energy. This is created throughout the day as we think, as we engage in activity etc. As an inhibitory neurotransmitter, it eventually starts to reduce activity in the brain, making us feel more and more relaxed and sleepy until we start to lose concentration and focus.

But if you keep drinking caffeine in large doses, then the brain responds by creating more adenosine receptors. It assumes that you have a chemical imbalance and it responds in kind. Therefore, you now find that you feel more tired and groggier when you aren't drinking caffeine and you need even more tea or coffee in order to feel alert and awake. This creates addiction and it is what leads to withdrawal symptoms when you stop getting enough caffeine.

In fact, it has even been suggested that what most of us assume is sleep inertia (the tiredness we feel first thing in the morning) might, in fact, be simple caffeine withdrawal!

There are so many more that do things like this. Consider for instance the role of omega 3 fatty acid. Omega 3 fatty acid is an oil found in fish that has two different benefits for the brain. The first is that it improves 'cell membrane permeability'. That is to say that the body is able to use omega 3 in order to create the cell walls. This, in turn, then leads to greater fluidity in the cells. The cells are better able to move freely, to change shape and to pass neurotransmitters and signals to one another. The result is that consuming omega 3 can actually help to enhance the transmission of signals across neurons and thereby speed up your thinking!

At the same time, omega 3 fatty acid also has the benefit of improving your omega 3:6 ratio. To simplify: omega 3 and 6 are both necessary for healthy function but the vast majority of us get too much of the latter and not enough of the former. That's because omega 6 is used as a preservative in a vast range of different things we eat, whereas you mainly get omega 3 from oily fish – which is absent from many of our diets. When you have too much 6 and not enough 3, this causes brain inflammation and inflammation has been linked with depression, brain fog and more!

How about creatine? Creatine is a substance that is typically associated with fitness and athletic activity. This supplement is used to enable the body to 'recycle' ATP. ATP is adenosine triphosphate, or the most basic form of energy useable by the cells. We need ATP to move our muscles but we also need it in order to think, or to do just about anything else.

When we use ATP, it becomes AMP and ADPT (adenosine monophosphate and adenosine diphosphate). Creatine recombines these two substances to create more ATP for further use, thereby providing the brain with additional energy. This is very beneficial and has even been shown in studies to raise IQ!

Then there are things like garlic or vinpocetine. These substances act as vasodilators, which is to say that they actually expand the width of the veins and the arteries, thereby enhancing blood flow around the body and improving the delivery of nutrients to the brain and to the muscles. This means you'll feel more awake and more focussed because you'll be getting more energy to the brain. On top of that, nutrients will also make it to the brain more effectively.

There are countless more examples of this. Everything from CoQ10, to resveratrol, to vitamin C, to magnesium, to zinc... countless nutrients, minerals and vitamins can enhance brain function in different ways. And conversely, eating too many ready meals and too much junk can actually damage your brain function and cause it to start becoming slow and sluggish due to low energy, due to inflammation and more.

So, eating right is one of the simplest but also one of THE most powerful things you can do to enhance your brain function. And by that, I mean avoiding processed foods that are low on nutrition and high on additives and meanwhile gravitating toward nutrient dense foods. Anything that you consider a 'super food' can potentially be very effective when it comes to enhancing your brain function and awareness, so make sure that you are eating a healthy diet if you want to make the most of your brain.

Meanwhile, try to ensure that you seek out these nutrients in particular:

- Omega 3

- Choline (found in eggs)
- Amino acids (protein)
- Vitamin B Complex
- Vitamin C
- Vitamin D
- Lutein
- Magnesium
- Zinc

Brain training is actually big business. You don't need to look far at all to find apps, games and books that promise to be able to improve your IQ and make you smarter through brain training. Very often, these involve completing strange puzzles, playing unusual games or performing math.

The rules of brain plasticity make it very easy for us to work out what impact a certain type of training will have on the brain. And we can actually use an acronym to work this out: SAID.

SAID stands for 'Specific Adaptations to Imposed Demands'. This is to say that your brain becomes better at doing the things you make it do regularly.

That means that the best form of brain training to become better at focussing on your work, is to simply force yourself to focus on your work more. Do this often and over time, you will become better at doing it. Want to become better at math? Then practice math more.

There are some tasks though that will help you to improve your brain in a much more 'non-specific' way. These involve activities that have changing circumstances but require the same basic 'skills'.

And a surprise one? Computer games. Computer games are actually among the very best brain training tools out there. In a moment, we'll see that they can be useful for enhancing brain plasticity, simply because every new game requires you to learn new inputs, new rules and new environments. But beyond this even, computer games are useful for just encouraging development in several key brain areas because of the skills that they require.

Action games, for instance, have been shown to increase our ability to tell different shades of grey and actually to improve visual acuity. The reason for this is that shooters require us to be constantly looking at the screen for signs of movement. Likewise, these games have been shown to help enhance decision making and to increase the speed at which decisions are made, without negatively impacting on the quality of those decisions. Again, this comes from the requirement to be constantly making decisions as to which enemy should take priority, which way you should turn, which weapon to use etc.

The difference between something like a computer game or something like a 'brain training exercise', is that a computer game is a much more varied experience and one that is far more closely relatable to our real-world experiences. Computer games provide realistic context and settings for our actions and they challenge us in a dynamically shifting manner.

Similarly, taking on new challenges at work, reading complex texts and trying to learn new subjects and putting yourself in social situations that take you out of your comfort zone... all these things would be more effective at increasing your brain power than doing any mundane exercises.

So, brain training is only so useful when it comes to boosting your brain power and works best when you go about it in less than conventional manners. But what if you take the underlying physical ability of the brain that enables brain training to work at all and then improve on that? What if you enhance brain plasticity?

Ultimately, I believe that intelligence and even athletic performance boil down to two things:

1. Adaptability

2. Opportunity

By adaptability, I am referring to the body's ability to change in response to certain stimulus. In the case of the brain this means plasticity – the formation of new neural connections to correspond to new abilities and memories.

By opportunity, I mean exposure or training. Take someone who is a fast learner and then give them an intensive training program and you have a master musician, programmer, linguist or mathematician.

Likewise, if you take someone whose muscles respond well to training and give them the right weightlifting protocol, they will stand a chance of becoming a professional bodybuilder. If the natural adaptability is missing or the training program is wrong though, the individual will never become world class.

There's more to it of course. I believe that true genius is more a matter of creativity than mastery. And I feel that the right motivation and initial interest in learning also needs to be present. But for the most part, plasticity has a whole lot to answer for.

So perhaps in that case, the best way to upgrade our mental prowess is to focus on that plasticity. By making our brains more adaptable, we then unlock the potential to learn faster and more efficiently and to thereby become smarter. We'll more quickly adapt to the mental demands of our surroundings and thus become better at thriving under those conditions.

And it's true that with great plasticity comes amazing potential. Just look at individuals like Ben Underwood, who can use a form of 'sonar' for navigation. Ben lost his sight at the age of three and his brain adapted to the point where he was able to find his way around using clicks from his tongue.

Imagine if you didn't have to lose your eyes to gain that kind of plasticity?

Potentially you could learn other incredible skills much faster – perhaps you could become truly ambidextrous, develop savant-like maths skills, gain useful synaesthesia or learn to climb like Jyoti Raju, the 'Monkey King'. You could maybe redesign your brain to your liking, just as a bodybuilder redesigns their body.

Many of us believe that our brains are most plastic when we are children due to biological differences. It's as though our brain's 'switch off' their plasticity once we reach a certain age and as such, we begin to find learning more difficult. You can't teach old dogs new tricks, and all that.

My argument though is that it seems more likely this correlation works the other way around. We stop learning and thus our brains become less plastic.

Studies show us that learning any new subject makes our brain more plastic. If you learn a language or study a new programming language for instance, you will begin to produce more BDNF – brain-derived neurotrophic factor.

Now think about what it's like to be a child: you are constantly flooded with new information and forced to learn everything. I'm not just talking about learning English, I'm talking about learning how to balance and walk. Learning what a human is. Learning that objects make sounds. Learning to make use of all your senses in a cohesive manner…

And the same thing happens to someone who loses their vision – they are plunged into a different kind of reality where new rules apply, reawakening some of that dormant neuroplasticity.

You'll never be as plastic as you were as a child, because you'll never be forced to deal with that much new information again.

I do believe that it would be possible to come close with some kind of virtual reality program. Virtual reality has the ability to subject us to entirely new realities, which could flood our senses with just as much novel stimuli as we experienced as infants.

This is why I believe that virtual reality has a very important role for the future of brain training.

But in the meantime, what else can you do to promote plasticity?

Learning

The first part of a protocol designed to enhance brain function would have to involve continual learning. I believe that this is one of the best ways to prevent age-related cognitive decline, to promote a good mood and generally to enhance brain health.

The problem is that many of us learn less and less as we age. After we leave that highly plastic childhood, we enter a stage where we are constantly learning through school and through social interactions. Following that, we learn to drive, we may go through higher education and we'll develop ourselves through our careers.

But come a certain age, our learning begins to slow down. There is less for us to learn and less for us to discover. Many of us find ourselves falling into a 'rut' where our jobs involve repeating the same few actions and our social interactions are limited to the same few friends and family.

This is why you need to actively keep introducing new learning opportunities and keep reaching for things outside of your understanding. This can be done through your career or it can be done as a hobby. Don't just focus on getting better at one hobby, focus on expanding your repertoire of skill and knowledge. You'll not only become a polymath through force of will, but the continual learning will ensure it remains easy for you to pick up other new skills as the need arises.

To encourage this, assign yourself a period of time every week to learn something new. This could be programming or learning a language, or it could be learning to dance or even challenging yourself to become ambidextrous. Better yet, enroll in an online course like my video class called "Empowerment Of The Mind"

https://www.hypnoticsuccesshabits.com/empowerment-of-the-mind

Another effective smarter brain strategy is causing movement through some kind of strength training. This is one of the big advantages of using functional-type training and doing things like climbing, learning martial arts, developing new lifts. Our brain responds especially well to learning when it is physical — as that is what our brain plasticity was originally for. Challenge yourself with new movement patterns and keep yourself nimble and agile both mentally and physically.

The other method is through gaming. Yes — playing computer games. Every single new computer game involves learning new rules and developing new muscle memory for quickly utilizing the controls. Computer games are the best we have for experiencing entirely new stimuli on a regular basis until VR gets to the point it needs to.

So, add that to your protocol. Make sure you are working out, make sure that this incorporates new and different movements and make sure that you include cardio and weightlifting. Use your body or you'll not only lose the muscle, but all that neural tissue that controls it. Use your muscle in new ways and your CNS will get into 'adaptation mode'.

What are the best supplements for encouraging brain plasticity? There are a few that are of particular interest to me right now and which make up my current 'plasticity stack'. This is another category of nootropics that can actually be beneficial to enhancing your brain function and that doesn't just focus on making you feel wired all the time.

These are:

Lion's Mane: For increasing nerve growth factor, which in turn has been linked to increased plasticity.

Magnesium Threonate: Magnesium has been shown to increase plasticity. Magnesium threonate in particular appears to more successfully reach the brain, making it the best choice.

Turmeric: Turmeric has been shown to enhance plasticity. My favorite food is Indian Curry and it is usually loaded with this.

Caffeine: Yup, good old caffeine can also increase plasticity. It does this by enhancing dopamine, which is correlated with increased BDNF (brain-derived neurotrophic factor). In plain English, caffeine makes things seem more important and more interesting, which makes the brain more likely to absorb and retain new information.

Lutein: Lutein was shown a while back to improve the function of mitochondria, leading to greater energy and potentially a boost in cognitive performance. Turns out it's also potentially able to increase plasticity, particularly in the womb and during our development but also later in life.

There are plenty more and tDCS has also been shown to be effective at increasing plasticity (transcranial direct current stimulation). But as we're looking at a practical solution to enhance your plasticity, let's focus on just these few. You can afford to add this little stack to your routine and it should result in enhanced adaptability.

Being in any novel environment, discovering something new, or even speaking to someone new can help to encourage more plasticity in the brain. Interestingly, this has also been shown to be a trigger for accessing 'flow states'.

In other words, when you're somewhere novel or encountering something new, your brain 'wakes up' which encourages a flood of dopamine and thus BDNF. Traveling, talking to people with different points of view and trying new things will help your brain to stay agile and youthful rather than becoming barnacled and set in its ways. An outward looking brain is one that stays healthy, young and plastic.

Research is still being conducted into what happens to the brain during hypnosis and whether brain actually fires on specific levels or not and to what degree. This research is relatively new and ongoing so I have purposefully only mentions in this chapter what is currently fact for the smarter brain concept. Of course we all know how wonderful hypnosis is for guided relaxation and change work.

8 UNSTOPPABLE CONFIDENCE

Confidence can be created, wouldn't you agree? Even if outside stimuli and your environment led you to grow up lacking self-confidence, you can use the limitless power of your brain to create a reality where you never lack confidence again. Just as with anything else in life, if you want to benefit from confidence and self-belief badly enough, you can.

If you want to improve your life in every single way, then boosting your self-confidence is one of *the* best ways to do that. With low self-esteem you're going to find yourself feeling bad about yourself and everything you do will be less enjoyable.

At the same time though, low self-esteem is something that you will 'give off' to others. This radiates from you whether you mean it to or not and in turn, can weaken the impact you have on others. Looking to get a promotion? Low self-esteem will communicate that you aren't sure you can do what needs to be done to your employers and they will feel less confident about giving you that boost in responsibility.

Want to succeed in your love life? Low self-esteem sends a

powerful signal that you are not a good catch. Clearly *you* do not think you are a good catch, so why would that other person think you are a good catch?

This can eventually lead to a self-fulfilling prophecy. If you act as though you are worthless and if you don't take chances, then people will treat you as though you're worthless and you won't find opportunities. You will thus get further and further behind your contemporaries, and that will only *worsen* your self-esteem.

So how can you get out of this rut? What is the answer?

First, let's take a look at why self-confidence is *so* important and how it can change everything.

You know when you were younger and you fancied the boy/girl at school? You told your Mum and she said: it's all about confidence.

You probably thought that this was a lie: that really it was all about looks or money. Saying it's 'all about confidence' and you should 'just be yourself' is car bumper-sticker advice. It's a nice platitude that is ultimately just a lie to make us feel better about ourselves. Right?

Wrong!

Self-confidence really *is* what it is all about. I know some guys who are unattractive in the conventional sense, not wealthy and not in good physical shape either. Yet they get *loads* of girls and the reason for that is simple: they are outgoing and fun.

This is why 'bad guys' will famously get all the girls. These are the guys that don't care what others think of them and that do whatever they want/. This comes across as confidence and it happens to be *very* attractive.

The same is true for women. A woman who is a 6 out of ten can beat an 8 out of ten if she knows how to flirt (which comes from confidence) and if she dresses to impress (which comes from confidence!).

There is a caveat: if you lack *social skills* then no amount of confidence will save you. That is something else you need to work on (and you'll learn here). Otherwise, it's all about confidence.

The same goes for your career and the same goes for the way you fit in with your friends.

We all know people who are supremely confident and we know that they are highly attractive and highly successful. We all want to *be like* those people.

And the reason for this is that confidence sends the signal that you are higher in the hierarchy than others. In the dating game, we want to date people who we believe are 'out of our league'. This makes us feel good about ourselves and from a biological perspective, it is the best way to ensure our DNA thrives.

If someone has confidence, this tells us that they *must be* an evolutionary catch. On an unconscious level, we are drawn to them because we think it will boost our status. Meanwhile, though, someone who thinks nothing of themselves will be ignored and will be taken advantage of.

It sounds harsh, but unfortunately, this is just human nature.

So how do you go about getting that boost in confidence?

There are two different avenues to take and these are external and internal. External confidence is much easier to acquire but it's the *internal* confidence that will make the real difference to who you are and how you feel about yourself.

We'll start with the easier, shallower option and then move onto the more profound change we can make.

Shallow Confidence Boost

The first thing you can do to give yourself an immediate boost in confidence is to change what you can about yourself to align yourself more with what *you* think a successful individual should be. For example, most of us feel that people who are more attractive and smarter are more successful. One of the biggest reasons that we might feel bad about ourselves is that we don't like the way we look.

So, the easy step one is to fix that!

One of the best ways to change the way we feel about our looks is to make some kind large change. A makeover might sound like a cheesy way to give ourselves a confidence boost but it really does work.

The key here is to be bold and to change things about yourself that you would normally be shy to change. You want to make changes that people will actually notice so that when you walk into a room, heads turn. You want people to think of you in a different way than they did before and you want to *feel* like a new person.

Most of us can think of some outfits that we dare not wear but that we know look good on confident, attractive people. Guess what? You're attractive too and the only thing missing is the confidence. Wear that outfit and you'll *look* that confident and that will make you *feel* much more confident.

Of course, you should still be you. So, don't wear things you don't like or that make you feel like someone else.

But just try to get outside your comfort zone and perhaps surprise people's expectations. Likewise, take some time to *invest* in yourself when it comes to your clothes and your grooming. Spend a little more money on better quality fabrics, take the time to do your hair and to moisturize. If you show that you think you're 'worth it' then this sends powerful signals too.

And if all of this is beyond you, consider hiring a stylist! There are people out there who do this for a living and who can help you feel *amazing*. Women: consider going on a makeup course!

Now enjoy those heads turn when you walk into the office and *work* that look you have.

This latter example of confidence-building works because it creates a 'virtuous cycle'. In other words, one good thing is going to lead to another. You'll dress more confidently and that will make other people treat you differently. In turn, this will make you *feel* more confident and you will start to *become* more confident.

But if you want to truly upgrade your confidence, then you need to do more work on that internal feeling of contentment.

And you know where this comes from? It comes from learning to *stop worrying* what other people think.

This is what confidence really is. The most confident person in the room is the person who spreads themselves out in a way that isn't done to make them 'look more impressive' but which is done in a way that makes them *feel comfortable regardless of what others think*.

The imposing person is one who isn't afraid of upsetting someone with what they say. They aren't about to agree with the general consensus just so that they can feel liked. They speak their mind – while of course still being respectful to others.

So how can you get to this stage? Where you genuinely stop caring what others think?

The answer is that you have to know yourself and you have to know what's important to you. Spend some time reflecting and finding what your life's 'goal' is, what your true purpose is and what you want to accomplish.

Once you've done this, you will be able to start working toward that goal and focussing your energy on those things that matter to you. And once you've done *that*, you will be able to shrug off the insults or the opinions of others.

Are people teasing you for being short? What does it matter when your goal is to become a great writer?

Not sure if a group of people like you? What does it matter when you know who your true friends are?

Knowing yourself and judging yourself by your *own standards* will make you immune to the judgements of others and will help you to strengthen your resolve and your determination.

And now, you will become someone who is much more interesting and much more engaging. Your passion will be apparent in the way you speak and the fact that you *aren't* so worried about what other people think of you will make you much more enigmatic and interesting. People you aren't trying to please everyone around you, other people are going to start trying to please *you*.

And this is the route of supreme, bulletproof confidence.

Training Your Confidence

Like everything else, this confidence won't appear overnight. It needs to be trained and it needs to be practiced. And this works just like training for anything else: based on the SAID principle.

SAID stands for 'Specific Adaptations to Imposed Demands'. In other words, we become better at doing whatever it is that we often do. If you want to be more confident and stop worrying about what others think, then you need to subject yourself to things that you would normally find daunting and continually reinforce your positive feelings.

If you are usually too shy and unconfident to speak in public, for example, this is going to be the *perfect* way to practice your new esteem. Force yourself to speak up in front of people. Better yet, force yourself to *get it wrong* on purpose so that you learn to face the music. Remind yourself: it doesn't matter what these people think and the worst that can happen is that you bemuse a stranger.

Practice talking to people and striking up conversation and always remind yourself that it doesn't matter what happens. You are developing yourself into the person that you want to be and that is *all* that matters. You can even try joining classes – a stand-up comedy class or a drama class can be a great way to lose inhibitions for example.

And once you get a *little* bit of confidence like this, you'll find that it begins to grow and grow into something huge. Everything you do will be reinforced by those around you and each win will only give you more confidence to focus on *more* challenges.

Researchers have noted that confidence in one area can be transmitted to another area of your life. In other words, become confident in your ability to perform one certain skill set or action, and you begin to develop confident self-belief in other areas as well. Why should you foster a sense of self-confidence? Is being confident such an important thing? As it turns out, it is. Take a look at just a few of the many benefits of being a self-confident person.

- Peak performance ability
- An improved immune system
- A lower risk of developing mental health issues
- Higher levels of happiness
- Better health
- Improved social interactions, including healthy, stronger personal relationships
- The ability to overcome obstacles which were previously believed to be impossible to conquer
- A lack of fear in tackling new situations
- Career and job advancement
- The achievement of just about anything you set your mind to.

As you no doubt have encountered in your life up to this

point, there are speed bumps, hurdles and other such obstacles present on the path to any worthwhile success.

When you set goals and achieve them, you build confidence. This has a lot to do with chemical processes that go on in your brain that are a direct result of the fact that your cave-dwelling ancestors survived. When the earliest humans lived, they pretty much had only a couple of things on their mind; eating, and not dying.

The world was a perilous place. With limited resources (no electricity, smartphones, hot fudge sundaes or coffee), simply surviving just to get through another dangerous day was very difficult. So the premier goal on every human's mind was to stay alive. When several days, weeks and years of continued survival happened day after day, the mind of man created a reward process.

When a human successfully saw another sunrise, dopamine, serotonin, endorphins and other pleasure-inducing chemicals are released. The brain rewarded its human owner for successfully getting through another challenging day. This began a chemical reward agreement that the brain made with the human body which basically stated, *"Every time you do something good for me, and for you, that allows us to survive, I will reward you by making you feel good."*

Fast forward several millennia to modern times.

That same rewards process is still at work. When you set a goal and achieve it, consciously or subconsciously, your "happy chemicals" come out and play. Your levels of stressors like cortisol and other "feel bad" chemicals and neurotransmitters drop. This is an automatic and natural process.

Whatever you deem as important to your personal value system is highly regarded by your brain. When you take steps to stick to your values and achieve the things that are important to you, your self-esteem skyrockets. You see yourself as in total control of creating the reality that you desire, and that is a really good feeling.

> *This makes you confident when faced with challenges to your values and belief system in the future.*

You have seen yourself overcome obstacles and work through problems to achieve a desired result in the past. Drawing on those memories when faced with roadblocks to your goals in the future, you are filled with confidence that you will have no problem achieving whatever outcome you set your mind to.

No Goals = No Confidence = Low Self-Esteem = Poor Health

Most people think they have control over their emotions, and to a large degree that is correct. However, many emotions are regulated and influenced by certain hormones. Neurotransmitters like oxytocin and the previously mentioned dopamine and serotonin trigger feelings of happiness, contentment and a high level of belief in self.

Conversely, cortisol, adrenaline and norepinephrine create

major stress in your mind and body. Too much cortisol can actually suppress your immune system, making you more susceptible to infection and disease. Accordingly, when your levels of these stress-inducing chemicals are high, and the previously mentioned "happy chemicals" are in low supply, you don't feel very good about yourself.

Fortunately, setting goals and achieving them creates a wonderful ratio where your "feel good" hormones, neurotransmitters and chemicals are in abundance, and your "feel bad" chemicals hightail it out of town. You have no control over this process, so why not use it to your advantage?

Set goals. Even pursuing small goals trigger this positive mental and physical health scenario. Through the accumulation of more and more goal-achieving results, your brain recognizes that you are good at setting your mind to something and then accomplishing it. Your confidence builds as you reward your value system with actions and behaviors that reinforce it.

Studies even show that merely pursuing goals triggers the automatic release of the chemicals that boost confidence and feelings of happiness.

> *Even if you eventually fail in achieving a goal, your brain rewards your active pursuit of that goal.*

This is why high achieving people are not afraid of failure. They are constantly setting goals and pursuing them, because their brain rewards them for doing so.

Also, it has been noted that if you build confidence in one skill set, this leads to an improved level of confidence in other areas. The science doesn't lie. When you have no goal you have no direction, and your mental and physical health, as well as self-confidence and self-esteem, suffers mightily. The opposite is fortunately true.

You can impact your mind, body and confidence in a positive manner when you benefit from the chemical processes which occur when you set and achieve goals. Research shows that the biggest benefits of mental and physical health, self-confidence and self-belief occur when your goals are very specific, written down, and reviewed regularly.

Here is The Confidence Formula

Confidence = Goals Missed + Goals Achieved

Some goals will be achieved; other's missed. The idea is to learn how to define your goals in a manner that provides more success than failure.

Thinking about running a marathon now could lead to a self-defeating attitude. You get out of breath just looking for the remote control, so the thought of running just over 26 miles sounds like Herculean task. However, millions of other people have been in your exact same situation and became successful long-distance runners. You can too.

The key is breaking down the huge achievement of running a marathon into a lot of little mini-achievements and milestones along the way.

This is how any huge achievement, task or goal is realized. You can't walk 1 mile in a single step. For the average person, a little more or less than 2,000 steps are required to cover a 1-mile distance. As you take step number 1, you are not thinking about step number 2,000. But eventually, if you keep plugging away, all of those simple, single steps add up to 1 mile.

This step-by-step strategy to goal setting and achievement can be applied to developing confidence, even for the least self-assured individual.

Using FOCUS To Keep on Track

By using the FOCUS strategy (Follow One Course Until Successful) you can easily build a long string of small wins that lead to self-confidence, self-esteem and self-belief. You will be employing a simple 6 step system to setting and achieving goals, and using the FOCUS principal on each individual step.

Concentrate entirely on step 1 until it is completed totally. Only when you are content that your first step is complete do you move to step number 2. You employ the FOCUS strategy there as well, and with each successive step, and by the time you are done your goal has been achieved. You have become a person that has on-call confidence ready whenever you need it. Ready to get started? Let's go.

Step #1 Develop a Crystal Clear, Detailed Picture of What You Want to Achieve

What does confidence look like to you? What are the physical traits of a person who believes strongly in his or herself? What kind of body language and verbal communication characterize someone with a high level of confidence? What are the feelings, emotions and desires you will experience when you are supercharged with confidence and self-belief?

Any physical trip you take requires that you know your starting point and destination. You know where you are right now. So your first step in achieving any goal depends entirely on figuring out where you want to be. Establish an incredibly detailed picture of all the character traits and behaviors that will characterize your eventually confident self.

Create a very clear conception of what you hope to achieve with your newly established confidence. Why do you want confidence? What deep down desire do you wish to fulfill through becoming more confident? Spend a lot of time on this step. Every successive step in your goal setting and achieving process depends on how clearly you have outlined what exactly you wish to achieve and become by developing more self-confidence.

Step #2 Visualize Yourself Achieving Your Goal

Your brain loves pictures. Along with your other 4 senses, your sense of sight tells your brain what is going on in the world around you. This leads to physical behaviors and actions that create a set of results. You make your reality happen just because of visual input.

Use this powerful tool to your advantage.

Visualize in your mind exactly what you want to achieve when you become self-confident. Take the previous step to a higher sense of reality. On top of clearly defining what confidence will bring you, picture yourself actually reaching the goal you set. One of the greatest ways to utilize the power of visualization is through self-hypnosis.

Visualize your newly developed courage helping you achieve some goal or desired set of results. Whatever it is that you want from self-courage and self-belief, picture yourself reaching that goal. This success step can be used anywhere and at any time, since all you need to do is spend a few seconds or minutes mentally programming yourself for success.

Step #3 Associate Incredible Pleasure with Goal Achievement

You have clearly detailed and visualized what your confident life will be like. Now attach immensely pleasurable feelings to the achievement of becoming a confident person. The next time you go through the visualization process, you may be surprised to find that you experience positively euphoric feelings and emotions, by merely thinking about what will happen once you become confident in yourself.

How will you celebrate when your newly earned confidence delivers some positive reward? What will your joy feel like? Who will you celebrate with? What environment will you be in? Make this extremely rewarding level of pleasure as realistic as possible in your mind. Associate it with your goal of becoming a person that can draw on supreme confidence at any time.

The more pleasure you attach to being self-confident, the harder you will be willing to work to make that happen, no matter what.

Step #4 Harness the Pain of Failure

Now you are going to do the same thing you did in the last goal achievement step. This time though, you will instead associate incredible pain with failure. Ask yourself what pains and other negatives can be associated with failing to achieve your goal of developing self-confidence.

What will you not have in your life? What negative emotions and self-doubts will you have if you don't develop confidence? Attach immense pain to the idea of never becoming a confident person. Professional salespeople and copywriters will tell you that there are only 2 root emotions which drive all human behavior – 1) avoiding pain and 2) receiving pleasure.

> Of those two incredibly motivational emotions, a person will seek to avoid pain before they attempt to receive pleasure.

You are using this psychological fact to ensure that you become confident at all costs, because you have programmed your mind to associate incredible pain with a lack of self-confidence.

Step #5 Identify And Complete a Daily Action That Helps You Reach Your Goal

Every day you fail to take action in developing confidence is a day that reverses any progress you have made up to that point. Accordingly, each and every day needs to involve some activity or group of activities which make you feel more confident and self-assured. This could include a self-esteem boosting pep talk every morning, spending a few minutes each day on the visualization process mentioned earlier, or engaging in some other behavior that cranks up your confidence.

You are not allowed to take off days when you are tired, busy or making any other excuse for not becoming a supremely confident individual. Results require action, and in this case, daily action. These are the daily equivalent of the simple, individual steps which, when strung together, create a 2,000 step, 1-mile journey.

Step #6 Make Your Goal the Premier Focus of Your Mind

People talk about keeping a goal or important thought "front and center" in your mind. This actually has something to do with the area of the human brain that deals with taking action, achieving results and reaching goals.

Your prefrontal cortex is located in the center, front part of your brain. So when you keep your goal, no matter what it is, front and center in your mind, your subconscious is quietly and automatically working on achieving it, even while you are consciously performing other tasks, behaviors or routines.

Now that you have a proven goal achieving system at your disposal, you need to think about some major thing you want to accomplish in your life. Too often, people set goals that are easily achievable. As you can imagine, your confidence does not grow by any appreciable amount if you congratulate yourself for tying your shoes or taking out the trash.

When you do achieve some major milestone in your life, your confidence and self-esteem both blossom quite a bit. This is because you set a meaningful goal which was also challenging.

Push yourself. If you have a quantifiable goal attached to some particular number or measurement, why not double it? Make sure that your goal is attainable, but it should be just outside your comfort zone. That is where the greatest growth and achievement is to be found.

You now have a firm grip on how chemicals, neurotransmitters and hormones make you feel happy and confident when you set goals, pursue them and achieve them. In the previous chapter, you were given a powerful 6 step system that virtually guarantees accomplishing any goal you set. In a perfect world, that is all you really need to create your dream reality.

However, you do not live in a perfect world.

On your journey to goal achievement, problems will arise. Because you do not live in a vacuum, people, places and things that operate outside your control influence your life all the time. Roadblocks appear out of nowhere. Life routinely throws you a curve ball, and your path to obtaining the things that you desire is put on hold.

This is why you have to understand how to effectively deal

with obstacles that threaten to keep you from realizing the reality you desire

Obstacles Are a Good Thing

If nothing got in the way on the road to accomplishing goals, everyone would have everything they desired. Goal accomplishment would be simple. You would set a goal, and easily achieve it. As you know, that is not the way of the world. Since roadblocks to success are so commonplace, and in some cases impossible to overcome, people naturally view these difficulties in a negative light.

That attitude leads to low levels of self-esteem and confidence, and fewer goals accomplished.

Obstacles are a good thing. They challenge you. They push you to higher levels of performance. Hindrances and hardships allow the cream to rise to the top. They can even create a stronger, more successful, more powerful and capable "you" than you ever imagined possible.

Look back at the times when you overcame some seemingly unbeatable stumbling block. At first, you saw that obstacle as an interfering mountain that you would never be able to climb. Through determination, taking action, and good information, you found yourself on the other side of the mountain, and clearing that hurdle was nowhere near as hard as you thought it would be.

This is going to be the case with most obstructions and restrictions in your life.

> *By remembering past experiences where handicaps to your goal achievement were successfully removed, you build the confidence to surpass any stumbling blocks you encounter in the future.*

That is just one tip that, along with the following obstacle-clearing best practices, will help you realize more goal accomplishing success.

1 – Be honest with yourself. Identify the things that are under your control, and the things that are not. If something is slowing your down in your pursuit of a particular goal and you have control over it, stop making excuses. Take action and do whatever is needed to clear that hurdle. If something is outside of your control, you are either going to have to ignore it, or brainstorm a unique way to influence it.

2 – Remember that everything that has ever been achieved by mankind was thought to be impossible at one time. There is a first time for everything. Before Roger Bannister ran a sub 4-minute mile for the first time, physical fitness "experts" said that the human body simply could not accomplish running a mile in under 4 minutes. Someone is going to clear the hurdle if you don't. Nothing is impossible.

3 – Set a time-frame for overcoming the obstacle. It's easy to say *"I'll do it tomorrow"* when faced with some distraction or impediment. The only problem is that tomorrow never comes. What you see a roadblock in your path, give yourself a realistic but challenging deadline for overcoming it.

4 – Look at the situation objectively. Step outside of yourself. Look at the reality you are in as if you are viewing it from the sideline with no feelings on the outcome one way or another. This outlook often presents simple solutions to what otherwise seems like an impossible situation.

5 – Begin to recognize obstacles not as problems, but as goal-achieving magnets. Think about it. Overcoming an obstacle automatically moves you closer to realizing the goal or desired set of results you are trying to achieve. This attitude makes you confidently positive that the next time you see some hindrance to the reality you are trying to create, you will have no problem overcoming it and moving closer to whatever success you want to realize.

Look at the people outside of your family that you spend the most time with. These are people you feel comfortable around. Unfortunately, they may be holding you back from your greatest achievements.

Human beings are intrinsically lazy. Our earliest existence was preoccupied with simply surviving. Today, most of us don't have to worry about survival on a day-to-day basis. We have a roof over our heads, indoor climate control, food to eat and other physical and mental comforts. So we don't try to "rock the boat", thinking that if we do, our wonderfully comfortable existence will be threatened.

We continue to pal around with others who are also at our lazily comfortable level, but that, unfortunately, means that 20 years down the road we will be just about who and what we are right now if we don't make some changes.

Why the 5 People You Spend the Most Time with Are Crucial to Your Success

Let's get back to some prehistoric references. The first cities and societies developed because surviving in prehistoric times was easier in a group than individually. Man was much more successful foraging, hunting and overcoming survival-threatening obstacles and enemies when he had others to help him.

Thousands of years of this behavior has created the social animal we are today. People are naturally drawn to other people. Science has shown us that individuals who remove themselves from society don't live as long as others, and experience disease and sickness at a higher than normal rate.

You can use this natural law of socialization to your benefit.
Jim Rohn was a successful author, speaker, sales coach and lifelong student of the human condition. He often wisely noted that ...
"You are the average of the 5 people you spend the most time with."

This means that financially, emotionally, spiritually, physically and in every other way the people you choose to spend your time with have a powerful influence over who you are.

Think about the people outside your immediate family that you consciously and actively pursue relationships with. Look at those people closest to you, and think about their values and beliefs. You will probably find that, on average, you are very similar to them in many ways.

> *Logically, this means that if you choose to connect with winners rather than losers, you can experience massive upgrades in your life.*

You should be spending more time with people who have accomplished what you desire. These successful individuals can act as mentors, speeding up your path to goal achievement.

Another benefit of surrounding yourself with winners is a marvelous boost in self-confidence. You see what is possible, you realize that these high achievers are really no different than you, and this fills you with a confident belief that you too can achieve the same results.

If you have been attempting to achieve a specific set of results and failed, this condition may have lasted for years, or even decades. Why is that so? Why haven't you been able to achieve the things that you think about every minute and every hour of every day and every night?

It certainly isn't because of a lack of effort or willpower. For example, dieters are some of the most determined and persistent people on the planet. However, even though they have tried several diets year after year, and worked very hard every time, they still have not lost the weight and kept it off. Logic would then dictate that a new approach is needed.

"The definition of insanity is doing the same thing over and over again and expecting different results."

If what you have been doing up to now has not produced the reality you desire, then you need a "reality reset". It only makes sense. If the person you are now is not the "you" that you want to be, stop thinking and doing the things you have up till now.

At the end of the 19th century the greatest minds in science believed they knew as much as possible about the physical world. Albert A. Michelson and Lord Kelvin, among other established and notable physicists, are credited with stating that there was nothing new to be discovered in physics. The year 1900 was rapidly approaching, and with the turn of the century came the recurring field of thought that human beings had pretty much realized and explained every major detail of our existence and the world around us.

You know by now that setting goals and building confidence go hand in hand. As you set and achieve goals your confidence builds. With increased self-confidence comes the realization that you can expand on your areas of excellence, creating and accomplishing things in other areas of your life.

This wonderful self-perpetuating cycle of happiness, confidence and success can be absolutely life-changing.

However, the obstacles are inevitably going to arise.

Sometimes, removing them is not possible. You simply have to give up on a particular path to achievement and adopt a new reality. This means recognizing failure as a wonderful life lesson, and not as a comment on who you are as a person. In other words ...

Failure is simply an event. It is not who you are.

Failure is only feedback, just like success. Failures and successes do not have any feelings about who you are, or what you can succeed and what you cannot. They are just results created by a certain set of behaviors and actions.

You are human. You are going to fail. That is an absolute rock-solid guaranteed reality waiting for you in the future. Since failure is inevitable, look at it in a different way than you used to. Smart people don't look at failure as a result, they recognize failure as a chance to become better.

They also take the time to express gratitude for the people that helped them get where they are, as well as those that helped them even though their effort may have ended up in failure.

Whether the pursuit of a goal ends up in failure or success, appreciate the fact that you made an effort. Pay this wonderful life experience forward by helping someone else overcome an obstacle or clear a hurdle. You were no doubt helped by someone to get where you are today, and helping others learn from your successes and failures will boost your self-esteem, as well as positively influence the individual you are assisting.

If you approach failure with the right mindset, as a wonderful lesson of what you should avoid doing in the future, and learn from your mistakes, you can gracefully move on with confidence in pursuit of your goals.

9 AVOIDING RED MIST

Do you find yourself getting upset with yourself or being bad-tempered and moody around your family and friends? Does the stress get to you and you feel like snapping? Have you been told you're wrong too many times on Facebook or had your opinion squashed? In the Military we used to call this "Red Mist" it is where you feel your emotion rising, triggering a rush of blood and adrenalin. It's that hypnotic moment where you just can't help yourself and you're about to speak your mind or lose control. As a Public Order Riot trained Police Officer we used to practice on the "Red Man" It was a guy wearing heavy red armor and we would practice hitting him and putting him under arrest. This chapter is not about violence, but it is about failure; criticism and when things are just a little off and you feel rattled and frustrated.

Our emotions often create mood swings in us and learning about our hormones and body responses to stress can be useful. However, often it's not our mood swings but rather its factors within our control that have created the moodiness in us and thankfully this is something that we can learn to control.

Learning to identify them and reverse their effects on our psyche can help us become happier and more controlled in our interactions with others at work and at home.

1. **If we don't get enough sleep, we will become moody.** Every adult should ideally have between 6 and 8 hours of sleep each night. Most people need at least 7 hours sleep, yet usually we find the time we have available for sleeping is getting lesser as our lives become busier. Increasing the amount of sleep will help us control our mood swings.

2. **Check your diet. Ensure you are eating a balanced diet** that includes plenty of vegetables and fruit, grains and nuts, protein sources and carbohydrates. Cortisol, a steroid hormone is produced when we are thirsty or hungry and this hormone reduces the immune system and increases our feeling of stress. It is easily reduced by eating and drinking and accounts for the feeling of well-being many obese emotional eaters feel when they eat.

3. **Engage in a whole brain activity, such as a sport** or other fitness activity to improve your feeling of well-being and reduce your stress levels. These activities have been shown to improve emotions, logic and ability to learn. This explains why women attending a gym regularly describe feelings of euphoria at the end of their work out session.

4. **Too much television and computer time can affect your moods**. The addictive nature of television and computers can create tension and anxiety when they need to be turned off or is interrupted, regardless of how important the reason. Morgan Freeman calls it the elephant in the room and single cause of all our problems.

5. **You yourself can be the cause of your mood swings**. Author Jeff Conley once said *"we must take a checkup from the neck up."* When we are feeling stressed or upset, we should try to minimize the damage by tuning up ourselves and our families and seeking to create a harmonious home for our families.

Timeout is a period of solitude where the focus is on self-development and self-reflection and removal of any red mist. It can be an extremely beneficial activity. When was the last time you treat yourself to a nice night alone, or a short trip from home? or needed to sit and calm the F%$k down

Sadly, most people don't take time out. Why? They either have family to take care of; crazy working hours or they just don't have the time to do it. Granting yourself a timeout is an act of self-renewal. This is the time for you to refresh your mind and focus on things you want to achieve.

Let's take a look at the benefits of making this a priority at least once a year;

1. Taking extended time out gives you the chance to take a step back and decide how to move forward in your

life. When you are in the middle of life and all its responsibilities, it's easier to focus on survival and not on achievement. Take the time out each year to achieve some life goals.

2. Timeout is not a selfish activity, but a time to be critical and honest about yourself and your life. The focus is to improve your relationships and to help your family and friends. It gives you the opportunity to evaluate what you are doing currently and how you can improve it.

3. Taking a few hours or a few days out of your busy schedule is not running away from your responsibilities. Rather, it is an opportunity to develop a **new enthusiasm** so you can keep *"running towards them"*.

Most people are keen to take the time out but struggle with how to achieve it. Here are some suggestions:

1. Discuss with your partner. Decide on taking the time out together or individually. If children are involved, try to get the help of grandparents, siblings or friends.

2. If you are doing it with a partner, try to schedule alone time during your retreat as well as time together.

Once you have scheduled a timeout, it is essential to plan on how to make the most of it. Preparing for the journey is as important as being there. Here are some suggested ways to prepare for your time out experience:

1. Choose a location that will help you to relax. Whether or not it is close to home, the key is to relax and refresh.

2. Don't bring anything that will act as a distraction. If you take your cell phone with you, try to borrow one that does not allow you to be tempted to check email or spend time on the Internet.

3. You can take a personal tape recorder (Phone app will do it) or a journal to enable you to record your reflections and goals as you create them.

4. If religion is important to you, take a religious book or self-help manual if you would like to use them as part of your self-hypnosis.

When you arrive at your time out location and begin the process of self-reflection, here are some guidelines to help you focus:

1. Evaluate what caused you to feel sad and happy as you review your life. These will help you to focus on things that need addressing in your life. What gives you that red mist factor.

2. Celebrate the things you have achieved, and goals you have accomplished.

3. Create action plans for those things you feel sad or dissatisfied with.

Do you often feel life has left you short, that somehow you have been robbed of the right to be happy and content? Maybe you have financial or relationship issues in your life or you are facing chronic health problems.

There is no one on this earth, no matter how rich, famous or successful who does not suffer moments where they feel that life has served them a difficult basket of trials to deal with. Other people wear smiles because they have learned to deal with their pain and problems and focus on the good and not the bad in their life.

However, finding the blessings in life and focusing on it rather than the negative is the key that opens the door to contentment. Every person is a unique human being and is the product of their past experiences. The potential for conflict is always there when people interact with each other.

As we focus on avoiding red mist we also should observe the good in people around us and the benefits of our relationship with them, it helps us put a different perspective on the difficult area of appreciation.

Sometimes differences may be irreconcilable, but often-true happiness is not the same as perceived happiness and constantly comparing our relationships or our life with others circumstances will only serve to drag us down. As we learn this essential life lesson, we can learn to explore and find happiness where we least expect it.

Depending on which culture you were brought up in, you may be raised to be a good giver or a good receiver.

Generally speaking, if you came from an Asian background like Japan, you were brought up to give and think about the community and group first before your individual needs. There is neither good nor bad in it unless you are a good giver but not a good receiver. By the way, take your mind out of the gutter. I actually wrote all this with a straight face in my pajamas and housecoat.

People who only give but not receive will not fully understand the joys of receiving and will be unbalanced.

So how do you know if you are not a good receiver?

Well the question to ask yourself is, what gifts have you given to yourself recently?

Have you treated yourself to something that you really want?

Do you downplay compliments that come your way or do you agree and receive them gracefully?

When you are not receiving properly, it's hard for more joy and miracles to happen. The universe is constantly giving and wants to give but you must be open to receive.

Start today by fully accepting a compliment and believe in it. Start by treating yourself to something that you've always wanted and be happy about it. When you start receiving more and more you will realize that you are in a much better position to give more because you can only give what you have. So fill yourself up first!

We cannot always control our reactions to the behaviors of others, but we can learn to control the way we see and respond to them.

"If you keep your head when all about you are losing theirs and blaming it on you" is a line from Rudyard Kipling's famous poem *"If."* There are probably many of us who can identify with the words and understand the frustration of being misunderstood or unfairly judged.

Do you sometimes feel that your life is going in the wrong direction and it is out of control? When we face these types of situations, we have two choices. We can either accept that there are things in our lives we cannot change, and there are things in life we can.

When there are things in our life we can change, then we must not wait for things to change, but we must work at changing them. Many of us know that certain things in our life must change. However, we procrastinate on making that change to improve it.

If we leave it to be, it can control our lives. Francis of Assisi once asked for the *"courage to change the things that can be changed and to accept the things that can't be changed and the ability to tell the difference."*

The prayer of Francis asked for the ability to tell the difference between the things we can change and the things we can't change. This is the first step towards finding the solution to a bad condition. We need to ask if the situation can be changed. If it is possible, what are the practical steps we need to bring about the changes?

Having determined the answer to that question, we need to put steps in place to help us make the change. If we decide the change can't be made, we need to try to see the situation in the bigger picture. We need to accept the problem is here to stay and our goals must be on how to relegate the problem and value the life we have apart from the problem

Most people approach differences of opinions whilst other people attempting to defend their point of view. Our intention may be to defend our personal position, but most people view our defensive stance as attacking their viewpoint. It can create confrontation and easily leads to interpersonal issues with the other person. This approach to conflict resolution creates many avoidable arguments in the workplace and home.

So how can we present our point of view without creating this reaction in people? The key is to learn to see the situation from the other's point of view and address it from within their viewpoint as well as from our own. We can still express our thoughts and feelings about a situation using this approach, but it usually produces a very different outcome.

This technique is an excellent way to approach all communication, whether with family, friends, work colleagues or strangers. We learn to express our thoughts, concerns and ideas and even disagree with others, but acknowledge verbally and through our body language, that the other person has the right to their opinions and thoughts about the issue causing the disagreement.

This approach maintains a relationship between two people that acknowledges that no one position is more valid than another's views, perspectives or thoughts. This does not mean that both ideas are equally valid, but conveys the understanding that the other person has a right to the thoughts or opinions about the situation causing the disagreement. This approach values the relationship and validates the person, whilst not necessarily validating the problem or the suggested solution.

There is an old saying that states, *"you will never know another person until you first walk in their shoes."* Trying to approach and diffuse a situation from their perspective enables us to walk in their shoes in the situation. It changes the *"I want"* statements, which presents the issue from our perspective to the *"I know you feel this way and I can understand why you do, but may I present another idea or show you why that idea is not the best one?"*

As we learn and apply this technique in our lives, it becomes obvious we have gained insight into a fundamental life lesson that validates and maintains relationships, even if we don't agree with the other person. It helps us to approach potential conflict situations in a non-confrontational way that promotes discussion and resolution. As a Police Officer in the United Kingdom conflict resolution played a crucial role in staying safe while removing anger and conflict in many situations.

How people feel about something often dictates whether they do it or not, or enjoy doing it or not. They may even choose not to do something because of how they feel about it.

The issue with this type of reaction is that, it is deeply rooted in the emotions and not in logic, although logic and feelings may lead us to the same conclusion. This is what is meant by *"experiencing your feelings"*. Have you learned to tell the difference between *"experiencing your feelings and being led by them?"*.

Experiencing your feelings enables you to rise above your feelings then logically decide what action to take.

This is particularly important if you have an argument with a spouse or child. It is very easy to be led by feelings as the argument becomes more heated. A wise spouse or parent, on recognizing and understanding the increased feelings of frustration and anger welling up inside them, will suggest time out to give each person time and space to think and respond logically rather than emotionally.

Learning to differentiate between acting on our feelings and understanding how they can help or hinder our actions and reactions is essential to achieving positive thinking. Negative feelings can hold us hostage to ourselves and difficult to achieve our goals in our life. We don't feel happy or fulfilled with what we have, so we strive for more. We feel depressed so we isolate ourselves from others or we overeat. We feel angry so we take it out through our attitudes to our children or our spouse.

As we learn to channel our negative thoughts and feelings into more positive decision-making, we are able to use them to help us choose behaviours but we don't let them dictate our actions without first challenging them by thinking through alternative options that can positively affect our lives and the choices we make.

Many people try new ideas and when it doesn't go well for them, they give up and feel like failures. Others, after trying new ideas and failing, refuse to give up and continue to try and as a result, they end up successful.

Why do some people choose to make the most of the experience no matter what the result may be and others rate it a failure if things don't go well? The answer is an optimistic attitude to every experience in life. Successes are achievements enjoyed today and failures are learning tools for future experience**s**. *There are no failures; they are simply steps towards future successes.*

How to be Assertive Without Offending or Causing Violence

By nature, most of us are people pleasers. That is to say that we want to be liked and the easiest seeming way to do that is by agreeing and not 'making a fuss'.

In the long run however, this is not a good strategy. Because eventually, this method means that people are likely to start taking your easy-going nature for granted. It means that you're unlikely to get things your way all that often. And eventually, this all means that you're highly likely to start to feel a little resentment toward people.

In other words, it pays every now and then to stand up for yourself and to be assertive. That means telling people what you want, telling people when things have gone too far and generally being a little more *honest* about your feels.

So how do you do that?

Getting Attention

The first thing to do is to get the attention of the person or people with whom you wish to speak. There is a time and a place to make your stand and if you get this wrong, then you are only going to end up making things awkward. Suddenly announcing in a group setting that you feel picked on can make for a bit of a scene!

Instead, take one or two people to one side at a moment when you know you'll have some privacy and when you have more control over the situation and the variables.

Then make sure that they are listening to you. That means saying you need to talk to them and trying to hold their gaze.

Know What You Want

If you're going to try and change a situation, then you need to have a clear goal for what you want. Complaining or generally making a fuss can make you look a little emotionally volatile, which is not our aim here. Instead, go in with a clear idea of what you want and how you're going to get it. If you want your friends to stop teasing you with a certain nickname, then just ask for that. If you want your partner to start picking up after themselves, then ask for that.

Be Firm But Fair

Now is not the time to point fingers, to blame people, or to generally be confrontational. Take personal relationships out of the matter and remember to focus on the goal. To that end, ask for what you want and take the stance that the person you are talking to has made a mistake or didn't realize they were frustrating you.

Make Sure You're Clear

Finally, it's always a good idea to make sure that the person you've spoken to is clear on the situation and that you're all on the same page. A good way to do this is to ask them to repeat back to you what you've asked them to do, or to 'promise'. And make sure that they have your eye contact when they do.

Learning to laugh at our mistakes and to dream big dreams are two very important characteristics that optimists develop that enable them to look at something that some may call as a failure as a learning opportunity.

When we take ourselves too seriously, we are more likely to think of our failures as permanent and they often attack our sense of self-worth.

When we can focus on our other successes and see this as a setback that we can laugh at and continue to dream of success next time we maintain our optimism.

So how do we deal with failure so we can see it as a learning tool for the future?

1. Challenge what you think of success and failure. It's our perception of them that makes us see failure as negative and success as positive. Failure is simply part of the journey to success, the ultimate destination.

2. When you feel like a failure because of a poor result or outcome, set goals for yourself immediately, deciding how to continue your journey to success. The old, but familiar saying of *"climb back on your horse immediately after you fall off"* is based on this concept.

3. Look at a failure from the perspective of the big picture, not the small picture. You may have not achieved the outcome you wanted, but you did achieve. Make a list of all the things you learned and gained from the experience and celebrate those things. They are achievements, it is not one complete failure, but many small achievements and they deserve to be celebrated.

Failure is about opportunity and embracing failure as opportunity helps to eliminate failure from your vocabulary helping you to stay optimistic and find success in everything you do.

When was the last time you watched a bee as it busily went from flower to flower collecting the nectar and pollen that would become the life-saving energy source for the larvae back at the hive? While some bees are happy to collect pollen from many different plants and flowers, others specialize in only collecting from certain species. The honey produced in the hives of these specialist bees is highly sought after for its unique qualities and flavors.

When making life choices we can be like the specialist honeybee, taking the good things offered to us in life and rejecting the rest that will potentially harm us or our quality of life. Learning to say no is a powerful tool that many of us rarely, if ever, use.

Learning to reject or say no to what will hurt or harm us in the long term is the key to reducing the amount of stress we carry each day and to feeling better about ourselves, as well as the choices we make.

As we learn to reject the things that will harm us, we are more inclined to accept the things that will help us. How can you tell the difference between what to accept and what to reject to help you stay focused and happy? You need to identify the causes of your distress.

Growing through stress is sometimes not an entirely bad thing and sometimes we do need to move outside of our comfort zone to achieve progress in our lives. The key to knowing what will produce good stress and what will produce negative stress is to have a life plan and only accepting those things that contribute to it.

Do you know a person who is always happy and positive about themselves and life in general? They never seem to have a problem and they are able to deal with things in life with composure and grace. Do you wish you were more like them and you are able to deal with your life circumstances like they do?

These people have a way of seeing life as being the *"half full glass"* where even if things are going downhill, they find something positive to focus on. This way of viewing life is natural for some people, but for the majority of us, it is a learned response. It results from making an intention to look at the positive and to not to dwell on the negative.

Unfortunately, it sounds so easy but in reality, difficult to execute. How do people learn to focus on the half-full glass and not the half-empty one and remain positive? It's not easy to be thankful when faced with difficult circumstances. However, practicing gratitude helps us deal with the most difficult experiences we may face in our lives. It is the key to optimism and seeing the good in everything.

Half glass full thinking seeks to clarify a situation before complaining about it. It asks whether a complaint will make the situation better or worse and if it will help to resolve the issue. In most cases, the answer to both these questions is, no. A clear perspective on the situation can help us resolve a situation. Maintaining an attitude of gratitude helps us maintain a positive perspective on most things that happen in our life. It helps to keep the glass half-full even in the most difficult circumstances.

Don't be Trapped by Your Own Personality

What on Earth could I possibly mean by this? How can a personality trap you anyway? Ultimately, it comes down to the fact that many of us end up being a little trapped and limited by the impressions we want to give others about ourselves. We 'craft' a certain persona and then that persona ends up in some ways becoming bigger than us. It becomes the 'real' us and we find that we're unable to break out of that mold.

Human beings have a natural inclination to want to be consistent. We like the idea that the way we act today is congruent with the way we acted yesterday and the way we will act tomorrow. This consistency gives us a sense of continuity and suggests that we have a personality and a set of characteristics – rather than just reacting in the moment as a piece of biological machinery.

And when we are consistent, that means that others feel they can predict our behavior. They don't need to worry that you're going to suddenly fly off the handle, to be highly offended by something they say etc. That's Jeff! Jeff is always easy going!

Jeff loves apple sauce!

Jeff is such a democrat at heart!

But the reality is that people change. Over time, our opinions can start to vary and so too can our personalities. This is actually a good thing. Growth is normal and healthy and it suggests that we haven't stagnated.

Likewise, situations can vary. Some days we will feel great and some days we will get out of bed on the wrong side. Some situations will be just slightly too much for us to be relaxed about.

But sometimes we are so keen to be seen as consistent and we so badly want to be 'true to ourselves' that we feel we can't act in the moment. We end up pretending that we want to do something because it is more typical of who we are. Or we end up acting relaxed about something that is actually bothering us.

We feel stuck with one political affiliation because we've invested so much time and effort into it.

The irony is that we try so hard to be 'ourselves' that we actually end up *smothering* ourselves and acting like someone else entirely.

And this is why it's so important that you don't double guess yourself. Don't try to be 'you' and don't shy away from occasionally letting people down, occasionally telling people off, or occasionally acting a little differently from the way everyone expects you will.

In fact, sometimes it is *good* to let the world know that you're not always going to act a certain way. That you have a line that shouldn't be crossed. And that they do need to be *just a little* careful about how they act around you.

So the next time your barista asks if you want 'your usual' when really you fancy a chai latte today... let them know!

10 DIRECTION AND DETERMINATION

There are millions of people on earth coming from different regions, religions, colours and cultures. In spite of so many differences, one thing remains common; all of us have and need a **DIRECTION**. Again, the direction may vary from one individual to the other.

To discover yourself and understand your abilities to achieve, you have to understand the basic fact that you are bound to face obstacles when achieving your direction and of course you require a certain amount of determination to succeed.

For instance, when a baby is growing, they first learn to crawl, then they slowly learn to sit, then they learn to stand and then finally, they learn to walk and run. Despite the obstacles they face, the baby reaches their aim and successfully walks after many attempts and utilizing sheer determination.

Focus is another important factor related to direction and purpose in life. Many people do not know how to focus on a goal. They simply spend their time doing things that are a waste of time and without proper planning. Therefore, when you strive to reach for direction in life your utmost focus on factors that contributes to the achievement of your goals is critical. You have to exert sheer determination.

Do you remember the story of the Tortoise and the Hare? They set out to have a race and in the beginning, it was the hare that have easily bounded ahead of the tortoise and almost made it to the finish line. But this is not before the tortoise managed to go very far at all.

Yet, the hare was just a little too self-assured and he decided to sleep before crossing the finishing line. He slept for so long and so soundly, that the tortoise eventually crossed the finish line while he was still sleeping. Against all the odds, the tortoise had won the race.

We are often told that *"slow and steady wins the race"* and there is truth in that. What is interesting about this story is that both the tortoise and the hare were using their natural talents. They used them to the best of their ability. From the Personal Development perspective, maybe we should take a closer look and see what happened in this story.

The tortoise, while not fast entered the race with the best of intentions. He knew he probably would not win, but that didn't stop him from participating. No doubt, he went full speed and put his heart into the endeavor. He didn't just set out on a walk in the park on a sunny day. He fully utilized his abilities and in the end, it paid off and he won. No one was more surprised than him to find that he crossed the finish line first.

The hare likewise used all his abilities, and should have won the race, but he didn't. He had yet to learn the value of not having too much faith in his own abilities. He became so self-assured that he became arrogant. That caused his downfall.

When we compare ourselves to the tortoise and the hare we can learn some important life lessons that may help us in our endeavors. The tortoise did what he did best, to the best of his ability. He did not let circumstances overwhelm him, but instead he did what was asked of him and he eventually found success.

The hare likewise did his best, but he let the circumstances get the better of him and they did overwhelm him and he rested on his laurels rather than continuing to the finish line and he found failure.

It is worth asking if in our endeavors we find our successes by having the attitude of the tortoise, or are more like the hare, and rely on our reputation and this explains our failure to succeed.

It is not just enough to think positively. You also need to act on your beliefs and thinking. This is where determination comes into play. Decisions and the persistence and patience to pursue a goal relentlessly take strength and direction.

It is a great force in the world. Couple this with tenacity and purpose and you are unstoppable. However, if you waver at the first signs of difficulty, you will never achieve your goal.

Take for example, Nelson Mandela who fought for the freedom of South Africa and during his fight, was imprisoned for 27 years. If it was not for the sheer conviction in his belief and determination on what he was fighting for, was it possible to last for even a year in prison? Definitely not.

The thing is that determination is present in all of us, we just have to exercise it to be strong and harness it.

Here are 3 steps to increase and harness your determination.

1. **First Be Aware of Your Limitations.** List down an area which you like to improve on. Quite often an easy area is health and fitness because it is something which you can do freely and get results on when you are consistent. In that category, pick an activity which you would like to focus on getting results. It could be running, weight lifting or rope skipping. The next time you do an activity, measure your results and focus your determination 100%

2. **Push Yourself.** After measuring your results on an average of 3 times, the next step is to push yourself further. Stretch your limitations until you can go no more and go even further. So let's say you've run 5 miles in 90 minutes consistently for the last 3 times,

you stretch yourself by aiming for a shorter finish time. Set a goal, prepare for it and execute.

3. **Celebrate!** With each completion of your attempt to stretch yourself, celebrate your result even if it did not meet your goal. It may sound as if it does not deserve it but here's what happens. With each celebration, you are associating good vibes and feelings to the act of exercising your determination and stretching your limitations. And guess what happens when you truly reach your target? You celebrate even bigger!

We cover hypnotic goals and success habits in much more detail later on

With each morning that you wake up you are given a new chance at life again, to pursue and make life what it is to you.

Think about it. With each breath you take, you are alive and that means you have the choice to change the direction of your life completely and everyone has this choice. You are forced to do something. You always have a choice. Every second of your life is an opportunity, a choice.

So this means that each day, you have millions of potential opportunities; to be reborn and change your life direction. There is power in making a true decision at that moment.

To assist you in making this decision, I want to share with you the Countdown method.

This method is simply a proven way to assist you to make laser focused decisions and exercise your decision-making muscle.

How Does This Work?

Simple. The next time you feel as if you can't decide or you don't know what you want. Countdown from 4…,3…,2…,1…and decide. It's that simple. Follow your gut feeling and decide. This is effective because it eliminates overthinking and paralysis through analysis.

Do you find yourself focusing on the things you can't do and lamenting the fact you can't do them? Do you wish that you could do some things you enjoy doing better than you can do them? Most of us do have these thoughts and handle them in different ways. Some just continue to do them and some approach them differently.

So, instead of focusing on what you can't do, focus on the things you can do and work on doing them even better.

When we focus on perfecting what we are already doing well, we begin to feel good about ourselves. Every day we hear our self-talk telling us conflicting stories. Our friends may praise us for something we have done or the new clothes we are wearing, but we find it impossible to accept that praise graciously and without making an excuse for it. Our negative self-talk will often speak louder than the words of our friends. Focusing on the things we know we are good at, will help us boost our self-esteem.

Take time this week to enjoy and appreciate the things you are good at, particularly the ones you believe you can do well. Take advice from your partner or your friends if you are not sure where your strengths lie. Enjoy focusing your time and energy on helping the good become the best and then enjoy your achievements. Allow yourself to enjoy comments and appreciation of your work.

Think about your life today. Is it where you want it to be? Think in terms of your relationships, habits, finances, spiritual well-being and even work. All these things impact on the person you want to see yourself.

Remember, if you don't take control of your life, someone or something else will take control of it for you. As children, we were often asked the question *"What do you want to be when you grow up?"* Teenagers dream about their perfect relationship and young adults plan their next overseas holidays. As maturing adults, we need to recapture our desire and dreams.

Our thought process plays a significant role in our successes. Researchers have said that the concept *"We are what we say we are"* is a statement that we often want to admit. Our state of mind drives our actions. We achieve in life when we can visualize our success. It is at this moment our resolve, determination and confidence kicks in.

Don't let yourself spend time focusing on what you can't do, but rather on what you are doing and what you can continue to work on towards your goals and dreams. No one ever achieved anything without dreaming and determining to put the dream into action and succeeding.

It cannot be emphasized enough that your thoughts are your worst critic, but it is also your best ally. Your thoughts are partially responsible for your actions and behaviors and most people trust their personal perceptions on things that happen in their lives. Channeling thoughts to bring out the best is essential to reaching personal goals.

Surround yourself with people who will support your endeavors and ask them to help you counter your negativity. Nip it in the bud before it has time to blossom into something that causes you to lose your focus. Think of yourself achieving your dreams and you are half way to success.

All of us have something we really want to do but keep finding excuses not to. Maybe you want to start on a walking routine each day but there is always a house chore to do that *"must come first."*

Maybe you plan to take up golf, but there is always one more report to write for work. We are so good at making excuses about why some things are more important than other things, but the truth is, life balance means that prioritizing time for the things we want to do is as important as doing the things we know we must do.

We all know how vital a diary is and the importance of scheduling our time and planning to achieve the things we need to accomplish. In theory, we would love to execute each and every activity planned for the day as written in our diary, yet still, we make excuses at the end of the day when we fail to check out everything from the list.

When you did not manage to complete all activities as targeted within the day, write down the last five things you intended to do but didn't accomplish and state the reasons why you didn't accomplish them.

Be honest with yourself about the excuses you made to justify why you didn't do them. Maybe you felt too tired, or maybe you were fearful of walking that track alone. Maybe you decided to cook a nice dinner for your family instead of going to the movies.

Remember, excuses don't have to be negative. Excuses are really choices we make. Sometimes we make choices that are valid, other times; our choices are a reflection of other things going on in our lives. Therefore, writing down our excuses, is really about writing down our choices.

Why did we choose not to do something? Did we simply choose to do something else? Perhaps we were able to modify a choice to make it more achievable.

Once we know why we make the choices we do, we are in a better position to change our actions, attitudes or behaviors if necessary to make better choices. Our choices are the essential key to how well we prioritize looking after our mental, physical and inner health.

What can be accomplished in 5 minutes and how does it help our journey to self-discovery?

- Take 5 minutes each day to clear out some clutter in your life. Maybe a work area, a pantry or a garage. Allow yourself to enjoy the moment when you have completed it! Organizing helps us think more clearly and set our focus. Research shows that people with a tidy work area achieve more productivity than those with a cluttered area.

- Take 5 minutes to go for a walk and find something beautiful in your world you haven't seen before. It will open up a way to count the other blessings in your life that often stay hidden from view as we are often too busy to enjoy them.

- Take 5 minutes to do some exercise and marvel at how fit you feel today than you did yesterday. If you don't have time to exercise for long periods during the day, 6 sets of 5-minute mini workouts add up to a 30-minute routine every day.

- Take 5 minutes to pray, use self-hypnosis or have some periods in your day, where you reflect on yourself and your spiritual health and well-being.

- Take 5 minutes to fix a proper meal for your family and not find yourself too busy so you buy take away every night. Your body needs good nutrition.

- Go to bed 5 minutes earlier each night so you improve on your sleep cycle gradually. You need at least 7 to 9 hours of sleep to help maintain your focus and alertness.

11 HYPNOTIC SUCCESS HABITS

We, humans, are creatures of habit. We have evolved over thousands of years to like routine, to like predictability and to become ingrained in a certain series of events.

Most of us, therefore, have a routine that we pretty much follow every single day. Maybe you start your day by waking up, making breakfast, having a shower, getting dressed and then watching the news for 10 minutes with a cup of coffee before running for the bus.

You probably have a similar routine in the evening, which might involve doing a 10-minute shop at your local grocers, making dinner, watching some TV, having a shower and then reading a book in bed. You probably go to bed at roughly the same time every day.

This is no coincidence. This comes down to the entire way we are hardwired. The way our brains work and the way our biology operates.

Repeating the same actions or thoughts over and over again essentially means that we are repeatedly using the same neuronal pathways and causing the same connections to light up and fire. As we do this, those connections become 'myelinated'. That means that they are insulated by myelin sheaths, thereby becoming stronger and stronger. If you repeat one action followed by another often enough, then often they will become so ingrained as to become automatic and beyond our conscious control.

This was demonstrated perfectly by the psychologist Ivan Pavlov who managed to condition dogs to salivate at the sound of a bell.

This is also why severely brain damaged individuals who can't remember their own name might still be able to play incredible piano concertos. Some can do this despite even not knowing that they can play the piano! The simple fact is that the motor neurons are hardwired over years of practice. The groove has been greased over and over again to leave a final impression.

As for our biology, this is based entirely on rhythms and patterns. The sun rises at a certain time and this triggers the release of cortisol and nitric oxide. These neurotransmitters trigger a cascade of activity throughout the brain which makes us more awake and active. Then we eat and this slows us down slightly again and gets us ready for work.

After 4 pm, our lunch settles in and we start to become slower and more sluggish thanks to a dose of melatonin and serotonin. By the time the sun starts to go down, we are producing more melatonin and the build-up of adenosine in our brain is making it harder and harder to think.

If you get up at a different time, if the sun rises at a different time, or if you eat a bigger meal, then this can throw that whole routine out of whack and as a result you'll feel out of sorts. This is what causes jet lag and it's why one solution to jet lag involves altering your meal timings.

In short, the more we repeat the same behavior over and over, the harder it is for us to change that behavior.

If the behavior in question involves smoking, then this is bad news. But if the behavior involves going to the gym, then it's great news. I have been working out at least two days a week ever since I was 13 years old. That means that I've been doing something consistently for quite a few years. As you might expect, I now find it pretty easy to work out. Even when I am on the road, I am able to get creative if there is no gym readily available. I love walking especially, it's a part of who I am and it's no effort for me to go for a walk or do some exercise around my property. I have also been drinking beer since I was 13 and the same can be said, I enjoy it as much now as I did back then. I hope that gave rise to a cheeky smile!

In other words, harnessing the power of habit can be a powerful tool in helping you to get whatever you want from life: whether that's a better body or a richer bank account.

Before you can start the journey towards being successful and begin building habits that move you along that hypnotic road, you need to understand what success is. Most people only have a vague idea of success. This prevents them from actually becoming successful because they don't know where they are going.

It's like getting in your car and jumping onto the interstate with a full tank of gas, trying to drive to the perfect holiday spot. Odds are, you aren't going to stumble onto it by accident. You need a destination in mind, and you need a map to get you there.

That's exactly what this chapter is designed to be for you – both a way to identify your destination (sort of) and a road map to show you exactly how to get there. However, in order to start the journey, you first need to understand what success is, and specifically, what successful habits actually are. The goal planning and focus on it come later in the next chapter.

The reason that people have problems becoming successful is that they have not figured out exactly what it means to be it. That's why defining success is the first step in achieving it.

The problem is, success isn't really a destination. Success is actually a journey with stops along the way. Those stops are definitely the destinations that you want to arrive at, but there is no "final destination" that you will get to where you will finally be happy. When it comes to being successful and happy, the only way to achieve it is to be constantly moving towards your goals.

For example, suppose that you have the goal of financial freedom – being wealthy enough to afford some of the finer things in life. You may want to eat out at better restaurants instead of places like Chili's or Applebees (or fast food). Once you have created enough wealth to be able to afford restaurants where the bill always comes to at least $200, you are still not going to be satisfied.

You are going to want more, and that's okay. You set another goal – a higher goal – of being able to attend charity dinners where the price of a plate is over $800. Your happiness isn't dependent upon the actual reaching of that goal – it is based upon your hard work and your sense of accomplishment from achieving that goal.

The bottom line is that your definition of success should never be a specific destination, even though you should always be working towards that end. Instead, it should be defined as being on the path to get the things that you want, one at a time, and continuing to improve yourself and inspiring yourself hypnotically to reach increasingly more goals.

Changing habits is like getting out of your comfort zone and this is a very difficult task to undertake no matter how desperate you are. Most people have habits they would like to modify be it physically, mentally, spiritually, or even emotionally.

Habits become deeply ingrained in our minds. Changing it can really turn out to be a daunting task. To be able to make the change, you must focus on the behavior you want to achieve and not the one you want to eliminate.

Ever wonder why it is easy for some people to change while others just can't? You see, when you have that burning desire on your subconscious level, you are more likely to get it without having to endure much pain. The only way to execute change it is to look back at the issues that may have been affecting your perception in terms of your behavior. This will help both your conscious and subconscious work in harmony to produce a great achievement.

Write and rewrite your perceptions that limit you from being a better version of you. Once you have the behavior that needs change, then we can look at how to initiate and maintain a change;

1. **Pre-contemplation:** Here the person has yet to uncover their problem and they may try to avoid the subject

2. **Contemplation:** A person is aware of their problem but unsure if they want to make a change. They realize they should have done things differently but don't.

3. **Preparation:** A person is ready to make the changes, they are not completely willing to, but they are ready to change. Mostly this stage is entered when change is unbearable.

4. **Action:** Now, at this stage, the person gets ready to make changes.

5. **Maintenance:** The affected person has to learn to maintain the changes and be cautious not to relapse

or else they will have to go through the stages all over again.

But have you experienced that even after all the contemplation, the habit that you tried to change is blocked by something deep inside you? You have sought help from counselors, psychologists and spent money to every self-help seminar, only to find yourself at the same position you were in before?

This is because our habits monopolize our lives. That is why it is important to be aware of our bad habits and replace them with constructive habits. If you have yet to achieve your goal, then you ought to really examine your approaches to life.

I suggest you prepare a list of how you perceive things around you or your attitude toward life. Of course, you will have those that do not serve you well and you don't have to beat yourself down because of it.

All you have to do is eliminate them completely and replace them with their opposite ones. Whatever your perception is, your subconscious takes it in and it will become a self-fulfilling prophecy.

So instead of saying disheartening things to yourself or the situation you are in, think of the past achievements or think of how much you can achieve and how easy life is if only you apply the right skills. You may not believe it initially, but I advise you to keep doing it to the point of acting as if no matter how long it takes. People who know me know the difference of faking it until you making and acting as if, I prefer the latter. This strategy is essential when you learn to become a Comedy Stage Hypnotist.

This exercise requires full-time dedication. Otherwise, you will easily give up. Keep the positive attributes coming in until it steers you directly into your dreams.

We often think of habits as negative things. Even though we would prefer not to do them, we still do them unconsciously. It is useful however to consider that habits can be both good and bad, and that good habits are beneficial to us, and just as removing bad habits are important.

Habits are formed in roughly three weeks. Changing our lifestyle, or eating different foods, or choosing to go on a daily walk will become second nature to us if we can maintain the CONSISTENCY. With discipline, maintaining the new habit will be effortless.

The key to developing these healthy habits is to move them from the conscious level to the subconscious level. They should become something you do without thinking. For example, you want to walk for half an hour before work each morning. Thus, it is crucial that you walk each day at the same time you've set. Nothing should prevent that walk from occurring. After 3 weeks, if you do not do the walk in the morning, you will feel as if you have missed something out of your morning routine.

In forming new habits, it is normal to have a weak moment when your resolve weakens. When this happens, it is important to focus on putting the weak moments "behind you" and start the process again with no hesitation. With patience, the consistency will pay off and you will succeed in forming a new healthy life habit!

That brings us to the framework for those goals that you want to achieve – your habits for success. The hypnotic success habits that you will be teaching yourself will result in the success you desire. Habits for success are clearly defined, well thought out and designed to take you to the goals that you have set for yourself.

In order to understand what a hypnotic habit for success is completely, you are going to have to set some goals first. But for demonstration purposes, in order to define hypnotic habits for success, we will be using some example goals. In fact, so here is a typical goal that most people at some point have set or will set for themselves in their lifetime.

Example: The Weight Loss Goal

Our first goal is going to be weight loss. This may or may not be one of your specific goals, but getting healthy, losing weight and reducing the risk for heart attack, stroke, diabetes and other health problems is definitely one of the most common ones out there. It is also the number one reason a person comes to my hypnosis clinic.

If you have a habit of eating unhealthy foods and avoiding the gym, you are not alone. When age 50 starts to creep up on people, their health becomes a primary concern.

So, suppose that the goal that you have set for yourself is to lose 30 pounds and eat healthier. You don't want to set goals or develop habits that are negatives. You want to create positive habits instead. The reason for this is simple: when you attempt to change bad habits, you are taking something away from yourself – something you very likely enjoy.

Instead, form and create good habits that will automatically replace the bad habits. That way, you are giving yourself something good and not taking anything away – at least in your subconscious mind. The difference is subtle but it really will make a difference. The mind is fascinating, my advice is to play its game.

So, when it comes to identifying habits for success for this example, let's start with what you don't want to do. Weight loss can be a complex subject when it comes to the detail. For the purpose of this chapter, I am just going to skim the surface so that you may understand the example I am presenting to you, rather than a full weight loss lesson. For more detail, you can order my "Lose Weight MP3" or the audio CD from my website.

Habits to Change (Negatives)

- Stop eating so much junk food
- Stop watching so much evening TV
- Stop going to all-you-can-eat buffets
- Lay off soda

See how all of those are taking something away from your life? You are removing things that you enjoy and that's just depressing. It will be very difficult to motivate yourself to change your habits because you feel as if you are giving up lots of stuff that you enjoy. But let's change those habits slightly and make them positive.

Habits to Add (Positives)

- Start eating a piece of fruit every day
- Spend 30 minutes in the evening taking a casual stroll
- Start eating at nicer restaurants with a healthier menu
- Start drinking more water (unsweetened)

Can you see how much of a difference this makes? When you are choosing new habits or trying to break old ones, you want to make sure that you are giving yourself something instead of taking it away. Even though you know somewhere inside that it is basically the same action, you can fool your brain into being more motivated this way.

Everyone has habits in their life that they have developed over the years. Some of them are really good for you and others not so much. For example, you might have learned to brush your teeth every morning and every night before bed. This will keep your teeth healthy and it is a habit that will give you a better smile, save you big money at the dentist and prevent a whole lot of pain and suffering (anyone who has ever had a dental extraction will agree wholeheartedly).

On the other hand, you might have developed the habit of procrastination. You definitely aren't alone. Everyone procrastinates to some degree, and some people make it a way of life. Procrastination happens for many reasons. Sometimes it is the fear of success, the lack of confidence in achieving it and sometimes, it is just a lack of motivation.

These are just two examples of good and bad habits. You have thousands of habits (good and bad) that you have ingrained in yourself over the years.

Understanding how these habits developed will allow you to see your own successes and failures more clearly and being familiar with the psychology behind habits will give you an objective perspective and allow you to fix problems without as much emotional baggage.

It all starts with understanding the psychology behind your habits: how they form, what motivates you to perform them and how they become a permanent part of your life. Habits reside in your subconscious mind. The first thing that you need to understand is that all habits – from brushing your teeth to recognizing and taking advantage of multi-million dollar business opportunities – are formed exactly the same way. The neurological process in forming habits is identical, and it doesn't matter if it is a tiny habit, a major habit, a bad habit or a good one.

Understanding this is actually one of the most important things that you can do because it immediately tells you something about yourself – namely, that if you can teach yourself to brush your teeth twice or three times a day, without even thinking about it, then you can teach yourself anything. You can have confidence in your ability to teach yourself any good habit that you want because you have already done it many times in your life.

While brushing your teeth may seem to have very little to do with starting a business or making another interest you have successful, the process is exactly the same. If you can do one, you can do the other.

Imagine that you are not in the habit of brushing your teeth. You brush a couple of times a week, but you want to brush at least twice every day. You probably aren't trying to develop this habit in reality but bear with me because it serves to demonstrate a very important example of how habits are formed.

Let's start with the morning. When you get up in the morning, you know that you may have morning breath. The last thing that you want to do is leave the house with dragon breath and then go to work and talk to co-workers.

That's why when you first wake up, you are going to spend a few minutes thinking about what it would be like to go into work with bad breath. Imagine the look on your co-worker's faces and how people would talk about you. If you don't have colleagues like me, it will be the next available person, like a delivery man, etc.

This should properly motivate you to get into the bathroom as soon as you wake up to brush your teeth.

If you want to motivate yourself in the evening, using the same example, then spend a few minutes lying in bed and thinking about all of the bacteria, sugar and rotting bits of food that is still in and on your teeth. You will want to get up and brush them before you go to sleep.

These pre-actions are called hypnotic triggers, and they are the basis of the neurological process that creates habits. When you have a hypnotic trigger, you motivate an action. You can create these hypnotic triggers yourself so that you do the action automatically, and it won't be a chore. It will be something that you actually want to do.

Creating your hypnotic trigger is only the first step in the process of creating a long-term habit. You first have to train your mind to hypnotically trigger the action and then you will perform it. When you do that enough times (which is where the goals plan outlined in a later chapter comes in) the action will become automatic and you will no longer need the trigger in order to remember to do the action. This hypnotic trigger can also be known as affirmations and self-talk programming.

It is just as important to be motivated when you are triggering an action as it is to remember to do it. Just because you created a hypnotic trigger doesn't mean that you are going to want to perform the habit. That's why you need to create a benefits list for every habit that you are attempting to form.

Use visualization to motivate yourself to complete an action.

When you can see the end result that you want in your mind, you are much more likely to make the habit with or without the hypnotic trigger. Visualization is a major part of hypnosis and change work. What the mind believes, it does achieve.

Creating long-term habits that will last a lifetime does take a little work, but most of it is right at the beginning and the rewards for doing it are actually pretty great.

If you are planning on changing your life and becoming more successful by stopping your bad habits, you are going about it entirely the wrong way. There is a much better way to stop bad habits and that's simply by replacing them with good ones.

Let's get straight into some examples so that you can see exactly what this means for practical purposes. This is a list of some of the bad habits that you might want to change.

- Stop eating so much fast food
- Stop binge-watching Netflix and get more work done
- Quit procrastinating so much
- Stop staying up so late
- Quit being so messy

Okay, so now you have identified some bad habits that you want to change. The problem is, if you start on the road to change with this list you are going to psych yourself out before you even begin, because you are going to be taking things away from yourself. The way that this list looks to your brain is something like this.

- Never eat those delicious burgers, fries and milkshakes ever again
- Stop having the enormous pleasure of binge-watching Netflix TV shows
- Work all the time and always be doing boring stuff
- Quit partying and never stay up and do anything fun
- Be a boring neat freak and be cleaning up all the time

When you are listing bad habits that you want to break, you are making your brain think that it's losing some of the most pleasurable parts of your life. This will make you battle yourself when you try to make these changes. Instead, you want to do something different, like setting some new habits that will add benefits and value to your life.

As before and earlier in this chapter here are some examples of some habits that will do exactly the same thing as the ones identified earlier, but will trick your brain into thinking you are getting a reward instead of being punished and having something taken away.

- Eat healthy for at least one meal per day
- Watch Netflix on the weekends

- Complete at least 5 tasks each week before they are due

- Start getting more sleep on weeknights

- Become more organized in certain areas (home, office)

As you can see, even though these give you the same exact result as your other habits, they are not taking anything away from your life – especially something pleasurable. Sure, if you read between the lines, you can see that watching Netflix on the weekends means that you don't watch it on the weekdays, but your plan isn't to fool yourself completely. You just need to trick your brain a little to get it to stop fighting you when you try to implement a new habit.

The number one factor that will determine whether or not you can achieve your goals is whether you believe in yourself. Any negativity, whether it is coming from the habits that you are changing or the thoughts going through your head is going to mess with that confidence.

When you replace your negative habits with positive ones, you see positive change in your life. If you are focusing on the negative habits then all you do is get depressed and overwhelmed because you see just how many negative habits you have that you need to change. This starts an all-or-nothing cycle that results in nothing but depression and failure.

On the other hand, if you are trying to add positive habits to your life, you don't have the all-or-nothing ultimatum. You feel good when you act on your good habits, even if you aren't perfect at them, and it makes an environment much more conducive to change.

There are a few things that you should keep in mind as you are working on changing your habits. These are truths that you should remind yourself of every day until you have them memorized and can refer back to them.

1. Everyone has bad habits that they are trying to change. Some people have a few more than others but that doesn't make them any less valuable of a person and the individual who overcomes more to change their habits can end up a much stronger person than someone who got there easily.

2. Whenever you find a bad habit that you want to change, think of a way to put a positive spin on it. Find a way to create a good habit that will squeeze out the bad habits without making you think that you are losing anything valuable from your life.

3. The most important thing that you can do when it comes to training a new hypnotic habit is try your best every day. Don't get discouraged because you had a bad day and didn't do as much as you thought you should have. As long as you made an effort, it is going to count towards your 30 days.

4. Remember, 30 days is just a guideline. Everyone is different and there is nothing wrong with you if you

need a little longer to make a habit stick. In fact, some studies show that if you want to form a truly effective habit, then 66 days is a better guideline. However, 30 days is a really good start.

5. Be flexible when it comes to training new hypnotic habits. If you have made a goal that you are going to study a new language for one hour every day but you cannot ever find a full hour to study, there is nothing wrong with cutting it down to a half hour, or even ten minutes if necessary. Try not to be too rigid and don't be too hard on yourself if you don't get it right the first time.

The thing that you want to take away from this chapter is that you always want to make your habits something positive that are adding something to your life. There are some great examples here of ways that you can turn a negative into a positive. These may have nothing to with your goals, and in fact, your goals may be so different that you might not be able to see right away how you can replace the "do not" with the "do" habits.

A good way to overcome this is by writing down the "do not" and then coming up with a list of things that you might be doing in place of it if you suddenly found that you were no longer exhibiting that behavior tomorrow. Keep plugging away at it and refine your habits as needed.

30 Days to a New Mindset

You can develop a habit that will completely change your life in about 30 days. This isn't just a nice idea, but it actually is something that you will find to be true, that is, as long as you do it correctly. You are constantly creating a new mindset without even realizing it. Sometimes it hits you like a ton of bricks and other times it is more subtle. Think of a time in your life when you realized that something you had taken for granted for a long period was untrue (or true in some cases).

It may have been something that you assumed about a friend or co-worker, or it might have been something about yourself that you only just realized. Whatever it was, it changed your mindset. You had a psychological shift as a result of that revelation.

It works the same way when you create a new habit; when the habit has become ingrained so that it is almost automatic, your mind changes and the way that you feel about the habit changes.

Just as an example, suppose that your habit was working out at the gym every day for a month. At the end of that 30-day period, many people find themselves actually looking forward to going to the gym and working out, and even missing it when they cannot find time to go.

That's because their mindset has changed about the activity of working out. Now, it is something that they enjoy and get pleasure from whereas before, when they first started forcing themselves to go, it was pure drudgery that took all of their strength to do.

That's the power of changing your mindset and it is something that you will experience with every new habit that you form and every bad habit that you replace with something positive.

Why does it Take 30 Days?

This is a really good question and one that science has been asking and answering for decades. To understand the reason behind the 30 days rule you have to understand a bit more about the science behind that rule.

First of all – and bear with me here – it doesn't take 30 days to form a new habit. At least, it doesn't take 30 days for everyone. The 30 days is used as a guideline because I believe that it is a good, solid time to develop a new habit (as long as it is practiced daily) based upon the currently available research. The speed of a successful positive habit can be much faster with hypnosis and by seeing a hypnotist or even using self-hypnosis. I regularly meet smokers who come to my office and want to stop the nasty habit. They walk out within an hour completely making the hypnotic shift into becoming and being a non-smoker. When someone asks me how long does it take to help someone stop smoking, I can confidently answer "The moment they walk into my office, or even prior to that" I am using the 30 days in this book as an overall strategy to success rather than a quick habit change.

Studies have shown that it can take anywhere from about 18

days all the way up to 66 days to form a new habit. This will depend upon what the habit is that you are attempting to master and your own ability to train yourself to learn it through a hypnotic success habit approach. Everyone you speak to will of course have a different view, I am giving you my 20 years of experience of what I have witnessed work for me and thousands of others.

One of the most important things that you can do when you are building habits during the first 30-day period is to keep it relatively simple. That means building just one or two – or at the most three – habits at a time.

This will allow you to concentrate on those habits and make sure that you are taking action every day.

As you become more experienced, you can add more and more habits that you are learning, tying them to trigger actions that you already do. For example, if you brush your teeth every night without fail then you can safely tie a new habit to this trigger action without putting too much pressure on yourself. But the first time you take these techniques for a test drive, you should stick with three habits or less.

Micro Habits

Struggling to floss your teeth every day, even just for those 30 days? Then in that case, you might want to try using something called 'micro habits'. The idea of a micro habit is essentially to hack the 30-day trial by finding a way to stick to your habit for that long much easier and then extrapolating the results.

Simply put, a micro habit means breaking down your new intended habit into something that is extremely easy and simple to stick to. So, for example, your goal might now be to floss just one tooth and to floss a different tooth each night. This is a two-second job so there should be no difficulty in sticking to it.

But as with a 'full sized' habit, you should find that this micro habit becomes deeply ingrained after a while and that eventually you find it easy to stick to. Now all you have to do is to extend that habit so that you're flossing all your teeth!

A more realistic version of this might be if you wanted to write a novel, in which case you could aim to write just one line per night. Likewise, if you wanted to get into shape, then you could aim to do just 20 press ups every day.

This works best if what you're doing is still useful in its own right. If you only ever did 20 press ups, then you would still notice some improvement for example. Likewise, one sentence per night would still eventually lead to an entire book!

Try to avoid a scenario where you might look at your micro habit and feel that it is 'pointless' so you can just ignore it.

The great thing about micro-habits is that right from the start; you are going to find you sometimes end up doing more. For instance, if you have set the goal of doing 20 press ups, you'll often find that you end up doing a whole workout anyway – the hardest part is just getting started!

What's most important though is that you have the option to default to the micro habit. The important thing is that you are keeping this as a part of your routine – not so much that the habit itself (for now!).

Context

Another tip for creating a new habit is to try attaching it to your old habits and your surroundings.

In other words, if you want to create a habit of flossing your teeth, then a good option is to attach this to a habit you already stick to: such as brushing your teeth!

Likewise, if you want to get into the habit of ironing your shirts, pick a specific point in the day for it to come after – such as making your morning tea.

This works because it connects the new behavior to old ones inside your brain. You have a network of neurons that fires whenever you make your morning tea. Now, when that network of neurons fire, they should also cause the new network – the ironing shirts network – to light up. The two are connected.

This also works on a practical level: you need to find a convenient time for your new habit to take place and you need to find a convenient time and place in which to do it. And you need to know that said time and place is always going to be convenient. You need to always be able to workout at this time, in this place.

I wanted to take up self-hypnosis back when I was a Police Officer a while back for example as a regular part of my routine. I struggled at first because there always seemed to be more important things to be doing and I could never find the right opportunity. So, what I did was to attach my self-hypnosis session to my workout session. I already worked out several times a week, so all I did was to say that straight before a workout, I would close my eyes and use self-hypnosis for just 5 (yes 5!) minutes. That's a micro habit that would never take up too much time and I'd always be in the right place to practice it (the gym).

Keeping your environment and your surroundings consistent is also important as all the things in your periphery can help to encourage your habit. This is why when trying to break a habit, the advice is always to change your surroundings immediately. If you're trying to give up alcohol for instance, or drugs, one of the first things you're told to do is to stop hanging out in the same places and with the same people. These have become associated with the habit – these are now 'triggers'.

But if it's a good habit, then triggers are a good thing!

The Power of Routine

One action is a habit but if you string these together, then you have a routine.

I touched recently on the practical aspect of stringing habits together and knowing where you will be and what time it will be when you do that thing. This is incredibly important for accomplishing goals and if you can build a routine for yourself that contains multiple good habits, then you'll find that you massively enhance your likelihood of success in all areas.

For example, if you are going to start a new training program then you must know precisely when you will work out and where you will work out. And you should 'hang' this new habit off of your existing routine and actions.

If you simply say you are going to train 'five days a week' then this is not good enough: you'll find yourself putting it off, forgetting or feeling too tired.

Instead then, find a slot in your routine where you can always make space. if you want to stick to a healthy diet for example, then you need to identify when you are going to make the food and how you are going to eat it. For example, you could find a local salad bar or a health food store that prepares meals for you. You could order online fresh ingredients that are delivered straight to you with instructions on how to prepare them. Nowadays there are many online ways to help you stick to this kind of goal.

Creating a routine is a powerful way to accomplish your goals then.

BUT don't forget that the value in life comes from mixing things up and trying new things. Don't let yourself move backward, or you will start to atrophy and stop growing.

Habits help you get to where you're going, but don't forget to enjoy the view along the way.

Complementary Hypnotic Habits

There is an exception to this rule in the form of complementary habits. These are hypnotic habits that reinforce each other. When you have several actions that are related, you can use them to trigger one another and you can add several more habits to your day.

This works best when all of the habits are necessary for you to reach your goal. For example, suppose that your goal is for you to get in shape to run a marathon in 12 months. Even if you are overweight and need to cut down on calories, dieting alone is not going to get you in shape for a marathon. Instead, you can use dieting, exercise and even stretching to reinforce each other.

You do want to be careful of attempting to do too much, even with complementary habits. If you attempt to do too many things in a day, you are going to get overwhelmed quickly and you may not be able to complete everything in one day, which can result in frustration.

Keep your hypnotic success habits simple and stack complementary habits on top of each other so that they reinforce each other. Keep the number of habits you are learning in a 30-day period down to a small handful because you want to train yourself for success so that next time you do a 30-day session, you will already have the confidence to make habits stick.

Obstacles To Success

Let's go over the eight most common obstacles to success, including a strategy for overcoming that particular barrier, so that you can stay on track and actually get your habits to stick, no matter what comes at you.

Barrier 1: Your Confidence

The first barrier that we are going to discuss is your confidence. This is something that you can cultivate by taking a hypnosis session, giving yourself positive self-talk or listening to an MP3 on SUCCESS or CONFIDENCE from my library of hypnotic MP3 downloads. This program will provide you with the tools that you need to achieve just about any goal or develop any habit, but if you don't have confidence in yourself to succeed, you are going to find it very hard to keep going. Train the brain with positive messages regularly.

Barrier 2: Your Motivation

Your motivation is a big factor as well. This book shows you how to motivate yourself using goals. These goals should be something that you really want in your life, not something that someone else wants for you. Your goals need to motivate you and keep you going when you feel like quitting.

Barrier 3: Your Plan

Again, the lack of a plan can be a major barrier to success. But this entire book is your plan from the 12-month goals that you set to the very hypnotic habits that you practice and work on every day in order to get to those goals. Use my printed version of the Hypnotic Goals Planner to plan your 30 days effectively to 12-month goals. You can start anytime and don't have to wait for the beginning of any particular year.

Barrier 4: The Naysayers

You are going to have people in your life telling you that you are bound to fail. Some of these people may even be loved ones or friends. Others will be jealous co-workers or others that you cross paths with. Don't listen to the naysayers. They have nothing meaningful to share with you and often, the only reason that they are trying to prevent you from being successful is because misery loves company.

Barrier 5: Financial Obstacles

This can be a major barrier for certain goals. For example, if you want to start a business but you have no money, no credit, no collateral and no prospects, you are going to have more of a challenge than someone who has those things. But nothing is impossible and if you want to success, you need to do some research and find a way to overcome.

Barrier 6: Health-Related Obstacles

Sometimes, your health can turn down a bad road and it can be difficult to continue working on your goals in the face of a heart condition, a disease like diabetes, or even obesity, which can make it difficult to move around.

The only advice here is that whether your health issues stop you from achieving your goals will depend entirely on how much you want to achieve them.

Barrier 7: Personal Tragedy or Difficult Circumstances

Again, one of the things that often stop a person in their tracks while they are attempting to be successful is personal circumstances. A tragedy in your life or difficult circumstances beyond your control can be challenging and you will need to decide to continue working towards success. I taught a friend recently that out of pain comes your purpose, yes Silvia I am talking about you and your amazing journey.

Barrier 8: Well-Meaning Friends & Family

Sometimes, your family and friends will become obstacles even when they have the best intentions in mind. Have you heard the cliché about the mother who wants to show her son how much she cares after she sees him suffering all day exercising and trying to eat right to lose weight so she prepares him a huge meal? I dated a girl who had a son just like this. He was 16 years old and asked me about advice on dating a girl he liked in school and how he could lose a bit of weight. I advised him to simply stop eating all his mothers' food. We would sit down for dinner and she was an excellent cook, she would serve one rotisserie chicken for her, her daughter and me and give the boy a whole chicken to himself.

Sometimes, family and friends will think they are helping when they are actually becoming obstacles and you will simply have to let them know that they aren't helping.

Focus on building you hypnotic success habits every day and train the brain through focus and visualization and you will empower your mind to be unstoppable.

12 HYPNOTIC GOALS

Learning how to set goals properly isn't complicated, but it does need to be done the right way. However, the most important thing that you understand about goal setting is that the journey is much more important than the end outcome.

When you have goals and you are on track to reaching them, you are happy. But your happiness isn't going to become permanent when you finally reach those goals. You will be more satisfied with life and happier, but you are still going to want to set new goals. You will never be satisfied, and that's perfectly okay.

So, you might be wondering just what the purpose of goals actually are then. You cannot be successful without goals, and you cannot form good habits for success without goals.

You can try to force yourself to do something habitually, but without a goal behind them, those habits have no power and they will not stick, even if you do follow the steps required to get them to become permanent. Your goal is not only your motivation; it is also your blueprint. The goal that you are working towards will put demands on the types of habits that you create and it will shape the way that you change. Making goals to effect positive change is something I teach my private hypnosis clients. Goals can be formed into the subconscious mind where habits then manifest and become automatic and like clockwork. Don't critically think in the conscious mind, just do in the subconscious mind and you will become more productive and successful each day in every way.

An Example of Bad Goal Setting

To understand how to write a good goal, it can help to first take a look at what makes a bad goal. Why is it that some goals just don't work out the way they should? What should we do differently to avoid this happening the next time?

Let's imagine for a moment that you want to get into shape. You're planning on losing weight and building muscle – which is a pretty popular goal that an awful lot of people are interested in accomplishing.

In this case, a typical goal might involve writing down the ideal body weight and/or measurements that you are trying to reach and then setting yourself a target – 3 months, 6 months or 1 year. And then you get to it!

But this is a goal that is destined to fail. Why? Because it is far too vague, far too distant and far too out of your control.

Let's fast forward two weeks, at which point you have hopefully been training hard for a while and changing your diet. Suddenly, life starts to get in the way. You find yourself bogged down with other things you have to do and you just don't have the time or energy to make it to the gym today. Or tomorrow. And Wednesday is looking tricky. So is Thursday.

But it's okay. Because you don't need to work out. Not working out on those days is not breaking your goal. You have plenty of time to reach your goal and it is up to you how you are going to go about making it happen. So, if you take time off today, you'll just put some more time in tomorrow. Or the next day. If this week is a write-off, then you can always make up for it next week.

And so it continues, week after week, until you get to the end of your allotted time span and you realize you've blown any chance of accomplishing that goal.

Or how about this alternative scenario? Imagine that you did put in the time and you worked very hard every day to get into shape. But the pounds just didn't come off. Maybe this is due to a slow metabolism, maybe it boils down to people offering to take you out for dinner too frequently.

Either way, you get to a certain point and you realize once again that you aren't going to make it. Even though you tried your best. So, what do you do? You give up, disheartened, and you leave it a long time before you ever try again.

A Better Goal

So, let's imagine that same scenario but this time write the goal correctly. What would a good goal look like if you wanted to lose weight and build muscle?

For starters, you should remove the time element. Instead of aiming to accomplish something in X number of days, how about you instead aim to do something every day. Look at the goal that you want to accomplish and then break that down into much smaller steps. To lose weight, you need to eat 2,000 calories or less a day. And you need to work out three times a week.

If you can do that, then you will eventually notice changes – be they big or small.

So instead of focusing on the end goal, set yourself a short-term goal. This is something that is entirely within your control – meaning that you cannot 'fail' for reasons outside of your control. It is also completely resistant to being put off or delayed. You can't 'work out today' tomorrow! Likewise, a slow metabolism isn't going to prevent you from eating only 2,000 calories.

Jerry Seinfeld explains a technique that he uses to make sure he sticks to these kinds of goals and he calls it 'the chain'. The idea is that he builds a chain as he completes his daily targets and this then creates an immense pressure not to break the chain.

You can do this with a calendar and a pen. So, every day that you successfully work out, you put a tick on the calendar for that day. This will then start to gradually build up a row of ticks and over time, you will come to feel proud of that row of ticks and not want to ruin it by missing one. You won't want to 'break the chain'.

Whether you use this additional strategy or not, the point is that you should write goals that are immediate and simple. Meanwhile, you can let the overarching objective 'take care of itself'.

Is Your Goal Too Ambitious?

There's nothing wrong with an ambitious goal. Many people say that 'dreaming big' can even make you more likely to accomplish your aim because it attracts attention, gravitates people toward you and helps get people on board. If you tell people you want to fly to space, you'll get a lot more positive attention than if you tell people you want to climb Mount Snowdown (a pretty small mountain in Wales).

This is why another piece of advice that often gets thrown about is to 'have visions, not goals'. Visions are abstract and they are grand. These are things you visualize and dream about, rather than things you write down and tick off. If you want to get into shape, then your goal can be to train three times a week, but your vision would be to become the best physical specimen you can – attractive to everyone and full of confidence and energy.

But while a vision can be as grand and extreme as you like, those smaller steps should still be small and they should be easy. At least at the very start these steps should be easy and this will then allow you to build towards your higher overarching objective. Think of this as a hierarchy. At the top, you have your grand vision for the future – something so exciting that it helps you to launch yourself out of bed in the morning.

Beneath that, you might have your 'realistic' version of what you can achieve with your current resources. Beneath that, you might have the steps you are taking every day to achieve it.

The mistake a lot of people make is to lump all these things together and not to consider the necessary progression from one stage to the next. This is the reason that someone who has never been to the gym before, might well write themselves a new training program that requires them to train for an hour a day, seven days a week and to do this on a diet of 1,000 calories. They'll then do stretching on top of that and start a yoga class.

Is it any wonder that we don't tend to stick to these goals?

The problem really tends to boil down to impatience. People want to accomplish their goals now. They don't want to put in the time or the repetitious work that it actually takes in order to get to that point. And they don't want the uncertainty that after all that work, it may not pay off.

But you need to change that thinking. Everything worth having comes with work and diligence and this is often highly repetitive and boring. If you want to get into shape, you need to train regularly and it takes years to get to a point where your new physique is impressive and 'permanent'. If you want to start your own business, well then there is a ton you need to learn before you even get going.

(Procrastinating on a goal is just as bad by the way though – which is another reason it is so important you have a concrete action plan!)

Think of this like a computer game. Computer games begin with a few levels that are incredibly easy and this is necessary to prevent you as the player from rage quitting. Your goals should be the same – if your 'level one' is a massive boss battle, then you won't be successful.

Lots of people get this wrong when they are taking up running for the first time. Here, they aim to start running long distances right away and losing weight. It's grueling, painful and unrewarding and it leaves them gasping and achy for days after.

What they should do is to first focus on getting good at running and on learning to like running.

So that means they should be running short distances, not running too fast, not running too far and generally not pushing themselves beyond a sensible point. This way, they can gradually start to like running and they can gradually find themselves running further and further without even trying.

And in fact, often it only takes small changes to get to the place you want to be. This is best exemplified by the

Japanese notion of 'Kaizen'. Kaizen essentially means 'lots of small changes that build up to big results.

For instance, if you want to lose weight, then it might be easier to look at small changes you can make to get there, rather than massive ones:

- Park further away from the entrance to the store and walk
- Stop drinking calorific coffees in the morning
- Swap sugary soda drinks for still water as your main source of hydration
- Take your lunch snack out of your lunchbox
- Eat off of smaller plates

These are just a few small changes that should be easy enough for most people to stick to and yet they can be enough to really sway your calorie total in your favor – eventually leading to cumulative weight loss!

Have a Clear Focus in Mind for Your Hypnotic Goals

If you ask people what they want, many of them will simply say they want to be successful. But if you ask them how they plan to achieve this success, they won't have actionable goals.

If you have random milestones that are too broad, you won't be able to reach those goals. For example, if you have a bunch of goals like wanting to be successful financially, wanting your business to grow, wanting to be able to level up in your business, those goals are so broad, so all over the place, that you won't be able to reach them.

Goals have to be broken down into actionable steps. They can't be so broad that they're one-size-fits-all. Those types of goals don't give you a roadmap. They're just contributing to your confusion and overwhelm.

If you say you want to make an extra $40,000 this year, that's fine - but what are the steps that you're going to take to get there. You don't make $40K overnight. You make it by taking the smaller steps that lead you to that goal.

You need to define these smaller steps that end up feeding into your larger goal. So instead of having a goal of making more money overall, set a goal of how much money you need to make each day or each week to meet that ultimate goal.

If you want to make an extra $40K, then you would need to bring in about $3,333 a month. Break that down by how much you would need to bring in a week, which is about $833 or about $119 a day.

That's what you focus your goal on because when you make that $119 a day, it feeds into the weekly goal which feeds into the ultimate goal. And it's not so overwhelming.

If you have streams of income right now that aren't moving you toward your goal, then you have to come up with a way to increase that income. You can offer an information eBook, for instance, or you can set up paid tutorials or start a members' only paid group. What you can't do is sit down and think about your goal, plan it and then do nothing to move toward it.

Wishful thinking or hoping doesn't lead to changes or results. When you set actionable goals, it allows you to have a clear focus and helps you have the mindset to reach them.

You need deliberate goals in order to have a sense of direction. It allows you to lead your life rather than to be led. Plus, when you have actionable goals, it lets you keep track of your success.

If you know that you have to make $119 a day and one day you make twice that, then you're ahead of the week's goal. And that will help if you have a shortcoming on another day.

You need to first determine what it is that you want. You can't set goals until you know what you want. These goals should matter or mean something to you. They should be goals that you're driven toward.

The most successful people I know have an underlying motivation to their goals. They want to be successful but many of them have a "because" in there. Such as "I want to be successful because I want to be able to spend more time with my family." Find out your "why," this is discussed in Chapter One.

Some people have an underlying motivation to be successful

because they know what it's like to struggle and they don't want to live the rest of their life that way. Your goals should be narrowed down to specifics. Name exactly what you want. Break the issues down so that you can keep track of the goals in smaller, actionable steps. It's important that you have these goals outlined with a way to track them. I have made tracking your goals much easier by using my 390-page Hypnotic Goals Planner. You can download a version or get a copy in print on Amazon at:

https://www.hypnoticsuccesshabits.com/hypnotic-goals-planner

Use deadlines for yourself. If you know you want to make that $3,333 in a month, then this allows you to be able to break down when you know you have to have a product ready - or take a step to get something out that will work toward bringing in that money.

These goals should be ones that are within your reach. If one of your goals is to make a billion dollars in a year, odds are really high that's not an achievable goal. So don't set yourself up to fail right out of the gate with a goal that you won't be able to accomplish because it's not realistic.

When you create your goals, make sure that your mindset is positive. Don't set self-defeating goals. An example of this would be a positive goal of "increase mailing list by 25%" rather than the goal that has a negative spin such as "find a way to make up for subscribers who are unsubscribing."

Once you've created the goals that are going to move you in

the direction that you want to go, you'll want to reinforce them. Look at them once a day. Put them in front of you to remind yourself that even if you don't see huge changes overnight, these changes are happening as you reach these actionable goals.

Get A Copy of My Hypnotic Goals Planner

One of the best ways to set goals that will show you what habits you need to form to achieve the final outcome is to use the YEAR-MONTH-WEEK model. This is a style of goal setting that is similar to the LONG-TERM/SHORT-TERM model that most people are familiar with. However, YEAR-MONTH-WEEK is a much more effective model in today's world, where we measure success in those clearly defined periods of time.

If you are lucky enough to be reading this in January, then you have a great opportunity to create a perfect goal structure. If not, then you have a couple of choices: either set your plans for "the rest of the year," however many months are left, or you can set your longest goal period over the next 12 months, no matter what month you start in.

Those goals for the 12-month period are your long-term goals. They will be the guide that you will use to create habits. Your 12-month goals are going to be what you are attempting to accomplish with the habits that you create and you will see how they break down into those habits shortly.

First, we need to set some goals so that you can see how the process works. Let's start with some simple example goals for the 12-month period.

- Learn a new language
- Improve website traffic
- Lose some weight
- Read more books

The problem with these goals is that while they definitely tell you what you should be working on, they aren't clearly defined enough to create habits from. So, let's make these goals something with a definite achievement point.

Goal 1: Learning a New Language

Instead of learning a new language as a goal (which may actually take you longer than a year) let's use something that you can actually measure. For example, suppose you used the popular (free) language learning website Duolingo.

Duolingo allows you to earn a specific amount of XP (Experience Points) each day that you study your language. It also tracks your learning so that you can know when you are 100% fluent. This is perfect for a goal because you can set a goal of becoming X percent fluent rather than the rather vague (and maybe impossible) goal to learn a new language in a year. As a side note, you should also choose your language.

Goal 2: Improve Website Traffic

This goal assumes that you have some website (possibly one that is making money) that you want to get more traffic to. This may not be your goal at all, but it is just an example to help you form your own goals.

In this case, your goal simply identifies your objective without a specific outcome. If you increase web traffic by a single visitor, you will have achieved your goal, and that's probably not what (the hypothetical) you had in mind.

Goal 3: Lose some weight

Okay, this is a common goal, but again, it's not specific. Lose how much weight? By when? If you don't have a clearly defined timeline, you aren't going to be able to make habits that allow you to reach that goal.

Goal 4: Read more books

You are probably getting the hang of it by now. How many more books do you want to read? If you are planning for a year, then you need to realistically choose how many you will be able to get through. You also need to identify what types of books you want to read.

Let's rewrite those original goals that we have identified into ones that will actually help you create habits, as outlined in the next section. Here are some examples of these goals with more specifics and a timeline.

- Goal 1: Become 25% fluent in Spanish using Duolingo

- Goal 2: Improve Website Traffic by 50%

- Goal 3: Lose 50 pounds, 8 inches from waist

- Goal 4: Read 20 Fiction Books & 10 Nonfiction Books

So, once you have some reasonable, specific 12-month goals, you want to break them down into 30-day goals. Remember, your key to success is 30 days of training a habit.

This is where you break down your goals into monthly ones that will help you create daily habits. Remember, the goals themselves are simply a destination. Now, you have to create action to go along with these goals.

Sometimes, you can create smaller goals that give you a much more manageable short-term achievement within a 30-day period. For example, if you were to use the goal to create more web traffic for example, you might have a goal during the first 30 days to evaluate your current web traffic, search keywords and the like. You can also set goals to research methods for increasing traffic.

In some cases, however, this is counterproductive. For example, if you set a goal to increase your Spanish fluency by 20% over a 12-month period, you can't really break it down into more manageable goals unless you plan out which lessons you want to tackle each month and this often backfires because some lessons are much harder than others and people get frustrated when they cannot reach their goal.

The bottom line here is that you basically want to look at each goal individually and figure out how you are going to break it down. The YEAR-MONTH-DAY system is great for using habits to reach goals, but just be aware that you don't have to worry too much if all you have is a destination goal – one that is specific and measurable – and some habits that will take you there.

Positive achievements and successes create lower levels of cortisol, adrenaline, norepinephrine and other stress-producing chemicals. This is how high levels of self-esteem and confidence are automatically and chemically produced when goals are set and achieved. Without specific goals, the human immune system suffers, and fewer levels of the pleasurable "feel good" chemicals are experienced.

Any big goal can be broken down into bite-sized pieces. Stringing together small wins on the way to accomplishing a major achievement builds confidence in the process.

1. Develop a crystal clear picture of what you want to achieve

2. Visualize achieving the goal

3. Associate immense pleasure with goal achievement

4. Associate slight pain with failure

5. Identify and complete daily actions that move you towards goal achievement

6. Make achieving your goal a constant and primary focus in your mind

Goals should be challenging, but attainable. Psychologists in 1908 proved that existing in a comfortable, safe environment lowers levels of achievement. Accordingly, stepping just outside of your comfort zone is where significant change occurs. You are encouraged to set goals that challenge the possibilities of what can be achieved, while still making them attainable.

Any appreciable achievement is going to encounter obstacles along the way. Hardships and hurdles should be seen as opportunities for growth, and also as success-magnets. Since overcoming a significant obstacle can be difficult, when it happens, realize that you are closer to your goal than you were before. What you previously may have seen as an impossible roadblock to overcome was not as hard to defeat as you originally thought.

The 5 Day Plan

Day One:

"You've started on your hypnotic goals planning journey! Congratulations are in order! Some people never make it to this very important step. You will achieve amazing success, never doubt yourself for a second. You can do this. In 30 days or less you are going to feel awesome, especially when you are doing these habits automatically and these first few days are long behind you, you are going to laugh at how easily you were able to overcome obstacles. You will embrace any challenges and work through them"

The most important thing that you need to remember on day one is that you take it slow. Sure, you want to work on your habits and complete them if you can, but the important thing is that you do at least one thing from each of the habits that you are learning and forming. You can work on improving a little bit each day, but it is vital to think about and take some kind of action on each habit you are working on, each and every day of the 30-day period.

If you happen to miss a day, all is not lost. You can simply do it the next day and make sure that you don't miss again. Be committed and inspired, visualize what it is you want to change or become. One or two misses may not keep you from developing your habit, but five or six just might. It will depend on you. If you skip a day, go back and catch up. You can listen to self-help hypnosis audio to help you get into the success mindset or learn how to perform self-hypnosis to help you begin to get in the zone of goals and success planning. I help many private clients in this area who have gone on to become extremely successful.

Day Two:

So, you made it through day one and you did the two things that were necessary to make these habits stick – you thought about doing something with them during the day and you took some kind of action on each of them.

Now, you are going to work on them just a little bit harder on day two. For example, if your goal was to make a habit of going to the gym and working out for 30 minutes a day and you exercised for 10 minutes on day one, then on day two you are going to go for 15 minutes.

Whatever you did on day one, you are going to increase it on day two.

Day Three:

Day three is another day when you are getting used to your new habits. Don't push yourself too hard on day three because it is this day when lots of people jump ship. Instead of trying to fulfill your goal completely on the third day, just do a little bit more than you did yesterday.

Again, using the gym example, if you worked out for 15 minutes on day two, then work out for 20 minutes on day three and then stop, even if you think you can go longer. If you going for 30 and you find that you can only make it 22 minutes you are going to suffer a disappointment – which could lead to a setback or an abandonment of your plan entirely. Most gym memberships fail when you commit to a 5 am gym visit that you cannot sustain every day within the first week. Be realistic and don't torture yourself. Follow this guidance in this book.

Day Four:

Now, you are getting serious about your plan. Today is the

day when you are going to make your first attempt at completing your habit entirely. If your goal is to work out for 30 minutes per day, then you are going to do your very best to stay at the gym and being active until the 30 minutes are up.

Don't worry if you cannot do it. This is sort of a trial run and you still have one more day to perfect your technique if you cannot make it the entire day. But if you find yourself putting off the actions that will develop your habits, sit down and remind yourself how important they are to you.

The important thing on day four is to do your very best to complete as many habits in their entirety as possible. If you can't then you still have tomorrow, but if you can, then you'll have a big head start on your remaining 25 days.

Day Five:

So, day five has arrived. You have been building up to this moment for the past few days and once you complete your new habits for this day you will be over the steepest part of the hill and headed for the downhill slope.

Do everything in your power to complete all of your habits all the way today.

If your goal is 30 minutes in the gym and 1000 words on your novel, make sure that you complete every minute and every word. This is the best way that you can enter the remaining 25 days of your challenge with the confidence to complete the full 30 days and learn the habits that you have decided upon.

Time Management

Most of us have things in our lives we want to do, as well as those things we have to do. Perhaps you want to go to the gym more often, or you want to read more books this year. Like most of us, do you find yourself wishing you had more time for those things?

Whilst time management is important to achieving these goals, some other steps must precede it. As you define these steps, preferably using a journal to keep track of what you discover about yourself, they will help you to achieve work and life balance that will enable you to do those things you want to do and achieve at this point in your life.

1. List Your Goals

All of us have goals that change regularly and that reflect other things going on in our life at the time. List your goals and prioritize them from important to least important. Include not only the goals you have to achieve, but also the personal goals you want to achieve.

2. List Your Daily Schedule

Although we want more time in the day, all of us have 24 hours. We use some of these hours for sleep and some of these for work and recreation purposes. List down your daily schedule and include the things you must do because they are a commitment. This may include work commitments or school sport commitments with the children.

3. Prioritize Your Personal Goals with Equal Priority as Work-Related Goals

Don't minimize the time available to do the things you want to do, particularly if they are contributing to your life goals or wellbeing. Include family time and other essential life activities that require your time and attention.

4. Keep to the schedule unless it is an emergency

Most people who create a daily schedule, keep to it for a while, but not long enough for it to become a habit. Habits take around 3 weeks to form, so if you want your new approach to work and lifestyle to be maintained, you must protect it at all costs. If you want to achieve your own personal goals, you must protect them at all costs. Eventually, the changes you implement will become second nature, but until then, you need to stay in control of your time management.

Why not take a life inventory and write them down in every area of your life that is important to you? Search the internet or your local library for opportunities to develop new skills or new knowledge in those areas you want to grow in. Ask yourself these questions:

1. What are my goals and dreams?
2. How do my goals and dreams fit into the circumstances of my life at this moment?
3. What areas do I need training in to achieve my goals?

4. Who will be the best source of advice to take control of areas that are out of control now?

5. Where can I find resources to help me achieve my goals and if I can't find any myself?

6. Where can I go to find the information I need in order to start my progress towards achieving them?

7. What things in my life need to change so I have time to achieve my goals?

8. What attitudes in my life need to change so I have the intention to achieve my goals?

9. With whom can I share these goals with so that I have someone to be my cheerleader as I embrace my goals?

Each of these questions help you to prepare insights into yourself, your ambitions and goals to create a practical way to work towards achieving them and embracing the life you want for yourself.

13 SELF HYPNOSIS

Self-hypnosis is a useful tool for achieving deep relaxation and in turn effecting positive change. Many people have made their living by overlaying this practical and useful technique with unwarranted mystical and magical rituals.

The incredible power of self-hypnosis can bring tremendous changes in your life. With the help of self-hypnosis, you are in control to get the results you want and you have the power to achieve the extraordinary things in your life. I was terrified of flying for years after a scary flight from JFK to upstate New York yet, in the British Army I used to fly dangerous missions. I knew I had to overcome this fear and I practiced what I preach and through self-hypnosis removed the fear, don't get me wrong, I still dislike flying but no longer have a negative reaction to it.

It is imperative to note that before practicing self-hypnosis a person should learn from a professional hypnotist or by using a prepared sound file, whether downloaded or on disc. The benefit of self-hypnosis is that it is self-induced; hence, there is no need to visit a hypnotist on a daily or weekly basis. This not only saves valuable time but also saves money, as visiting a hypnotist every week can cost a significant amount of money. It also gives you the power to treat yourself and be in charge of your own life. With my consulting practice, I will see a client for a few sessions and then afterward prepare them for self-hypnosis if I deem it necessary.

Self-hypnosis is mainly based on suggestions and through positive suggestions, a person can make significant changes in their life. In the case of depression and panic problems, you have to learn how to control thoughts and keep negative ones at bay. You also need to learn how to substitute negative thoughts with pleasant, positive thoughts. Of course, a hypnotist can actually remove the thoughts permanently.

Braid, in his book, 'Observations on Trance or Human Hibernation' provides probably the first account of self-hypnosis by someone employing it upon themselves.

Extract of Braid's Account of Self Hypnotism:

It is commonly said that seeing is believing, but feeling is the very truth. I shall, therefore, give the result of my experience of hypnotism in my own person. In the middle of 1844, I suffered from the most severe attack of rheumatism, implicating the left side of the neck and chest, and then left arm.

At first, the pain was moderately severe and I took some medicine to remove it; but instead of this, it became more and more violent, and it had tormented me for three days and was so excruciating, that it entirely deprived me of sleep for three nights successively, and on the last of the three nights I could not remain in any one posture for five minutes, from the severity of the pain.

On the forenoon of the next day, whilst visiting my patients, every jolt of the carriage, I could only compare to several sharp instruments being thrust through my shoulder, neck and chest. A full inspiration was attended with stabbing pain, such as is experienced in pleurisy. When I returned home for dinner I could not turn my head, lift my arm, or draw a breath, without suffering extreme pain. In this condition I resolved to try the effects of hypnotism. I requested two friends, who were present and who understood the system, to watch the effects, and wake me when I had passed sufficiently into the condition; and with their assurance that, they would give strict attention to their charge, I sat down and hypnotize myself, extending the extremities. At the expiration of nine minutes they arouse me, and to my agreeable surprise, I was quite free from pain, being able to move in any way perfect ease. I say agreeably surprised on this account, I had seen results with many patients; but it is one thing to hear of pain and another to feel it. My suffering was so exquisite that I could not imagine anyone else ever suffered so intensely as myself on that occasion, and therefore, I merely expected mitigation, so that I was truly agreeably surprised to find myself entirely free from pain. I continued quite easy all the afternoon, slept comfortably all night and the following morning felt a little stiffness, but no pain. A week later, I had a slight return, which I removed by hypnotizing myself once more, I have remained entirely free from rheumatism ever since, now nearly six years.

Coué

Emile Coué was one of the most influential figures in the subsequent development of self-hypnosis. His method of **conscious autosuggestion** became an internationally renowned self-help system at the beginning of the 20th century. Although Coué distanced himself from the concept of **hypnosis** he sometimes referred to what he was doing as 'self-hypnosis' as did his followers such as Charles Baudouin. Modern hypnotherapists regard Coué as part of their own field.

Autogenic Training:

It is a relaxation technique developed by German psychiatrist **Johannes Shultz** and first published in 1932. He based his approach on the work of the German hypnotist **Oskar Vogt**.

Salter:

The first major academic journal article on self-hypnosis, **Three Techniques of Auto Hypnosis** was published by the Hypnotherapist and Early Behavior Therapist **Andrew Salter** in 1941. He wrote an article describing the modus operandi of self-hypnosis, but couldn't get it published. None of the professional journals would touch the article. After some time, he sent it to Professor **Clark Leonard Hull** of Yell's Psychology Department. Hull is the author of the work entitled **Hypnosis and Suggestibility**, and is not only one of the chief oracles of American psychology, but perhaps the world's greatest oracle on matters pertaining to hypnotism. Hull read Salter's article (though he had never heard of Salter) and was sufficiently impressed to send it along to the **Journal of General Psychology**, of which he is an editor.

His technique was developed over the time of two years during which he tested the methods with just over 200 subjects. Salter described methods of teaching self-hypnosis by:

1] Autohypnosis by post hypnotic suggestions

2] Autohypnosis by memorized trance instructions (Scripted suggestions)

3] Fractional Autohypnosis (Part learning)

Salter's behavioral approach influenced by Clark L. Hull, was a primitive precursor of modern hypnotic skills training programs such as The Carleton Skills Training Program developed by Nicholus Spanos.

The main technique used in self-hypnosis for resolving problems, is inducing relaxation and suggesting to yourself that the problem at hand is not as bad as believed. Another important technique used is for deep breathing. Deep breathing increases the amount of oxygen towards brain, which helps your muscles and mind to relax. It also helps in following visual-imagery technique effectively.

Let us go for a simple exercise:

Stare at the hypnosis spiral for half a minute and then look away. You will notice that your vision will be distorted. Try staring at the hypnosis spiral for about a minute and stating some goals in your mind. If you are stuck for ideas, better to try the immortal words of Emile Coue:

Every day in every way I am getting better and better

The self-hypnosis spiral focuses your attention away from everything else. This self-rapport is the main benefit. Ten minutes of relaxing self-hypnosis is equivalent to an hour of sleep for its calming effects on your mind and body. In self-hypnosis, you are able to free up more inner resources for utilization. When you self-hypnotize, decisions may seem simpler, because you can be more in touch with what you really feel about something. New ideas may come to mind, as your subconscious becomes very creative when it is not distracted by conscious routines and expectations. Anxieties and concerns get dissolved because of them sinking back into your subconscious.

You actually get self-hypnotized every day. Think of a time when you are nervous about particular event. Were you not thinking it in your mind, again and again, visualizing what could go wrong, even when trying to go to sleep? More positively you may remember a particular goal, something you just know you had to have. You likely told yourself through accidental self-hypnosis 'I can do it; nothing is going to get in the way'. These patterns of thought can work for or against us in powerful ways, because you are effectively communicating with your subconscious during this moment. Self-suggestion is a very common and powerful force which has probably dictated far more of your perceptions and decisions than you would realize.

You can use images which make you feel calm and quiet in self-hypnosis. While in self-hypnosis and before waking, as a last suggestion, think to yourself the next time you practice, you will be even more ready to relax quickly and entirely, and be even more receptive to your own suggestions. Then suggest to yourself how confident, relaxed and motivated you feel in just a few moments when you awake.

You may find it useful to associate a word or an idea to the self-hypnosis experience. It will make your next sessions of self-hypnosis more and more effective. You can imagine yourself drawing a circle around your chair. Once you enter the circle you can sink into the relaxed state of self-hypnosis. You can also think of a unique word, which you can repeat to yourself. This associates the word and 'anchors' it to the experience. Then next time repeat the word to yourself to sink into the trance.

You can self-hypnotize yourself to relax, to have ideas or to set goals. If nothing springs to mind, you can simply enjoy the relaxed state and allow your mind and thoughts to wander upon whatever presents itself. You may be surprised at the things you begin to consider in self-hypnosis, when not distracted by your normal thoughts.

Normally, self-hypnosis sessions last for 15 to 25 minutes; however, you may last as long as you like. There is no harm or side effects with it. As you go on practicing more and more, your (inner) mind will suggest to you about the duration that is adequate for you.

Self-hypnosis is a self-help technique to overcome a specific problem in your life. It can help you get started on your road to self-healing and development. You can find your own solution with the self-hypnosis and achieve fast, powerful self-change from the privacy of your own home. I always use self-hypnosis before a stage show, sometimes moments before walking on the stage. I call it the conditioning of my mind and "Richard's time."

Practicing self-hypnosis in a relaxed environment such as in bed first thing in the morning, the last thing at night or a comfy chair are right places to start. As you get better and begin to trust yourself more, you will notice yourself exerting a higher level of creative self-control at any time. You will learn to intuitively enter a state of self-rapport where you know you can easily communicate to your subconscious.

The key to achieving a greater depth of self-hypnosis lies in the use of visual imagery technique. There are many people today using self-hypnosis in the realm of sports. Under hypnotic state you can learn so quickly because of time distortion which allows you to obtain the equivalent of many hours of study in a relatively short length of time.

Now we will learn some techniques which are useful for many people. You can mix and match elements from any of these techniques for your convenience. While practicing these techniques three simple things are necessary:

Concentration

Persistence

Patience

When you want to use affirmations as a part of your self-hypnosis session, prepare the affirmations you want to use before you start the session, as you don't need to think about those once you reach the deep relaxation state. Along with meditation and imagery, self-hypnosis can be used as a part of daily stress management routine.

Technique I

This is a simple technique for relaxing or falling asleep. With your eyes closed, think about three things that you can hear, doesn't matter how slight or where those things are as long as you can hear those from your place. Then think about three things that you can see, if you had your eyes open. Simply consider three things or perspectives in the room where you are and think about the color, shape, size of those things. Then think about three things you can feel, such as a slight breeze, a sensation on your back, touch of your clothing, etc.

Then repeat this process, thinking of only two examples for each sense, hearing, sight and feel. Then repeat for one example, each time cycling between the examples. If you are able to complete this, start again, soon you will feel you are entering into a new state of relaxation. Once you easily achieve this state, practice Technique II.

Technique II

Prepare your own hypnotic script to relax your body and imagine hearing it from yourself. Describe your breathing, posture and feelings of relaxation. Pretend in your mind that you are standing above yourself, hypnotizing yourself. You don't need to know hypnosis for this. Simply imagine what you think would work for you.

In self-hypnosis, if you want to create any particular feeling such as numb arms, it is better to think about a time when you actually experienced those things. For example, you can think of a time when you were lying on the beach, enjoying a nice bath or when your hands were so cold that you couldn't feel them. Here you can take advantage of the brain's ability to conjure all of the sensory information for those events, and associate those with your current experience. Mental pictures carry bodily experiences. This way you can use your subconscious abilities to your own advantage. Once you master this Technique, go for Technique III.

Technique III

When you feel sufficiently relaxed, with your eyes closed, try to become as receptive as possible to whatever you are experiencing internally. Try to think about any colors, shapes you can see in your mind's eye, think about thoughts that you come across at that moment, memories coming up, anything at all, that is part of the experience. Then try to consider where you are, who you are? Try to take a mental step back 'I' that is thinking, 'I can feel myself thinking so and so'. Then try to go one more step back, behind whoever is imaging you doing so and so. Further back you can go, within yourself, the freer you will feel from your normal restrictions and ideas. Then you can begin to make suggestions to your subconscious and try to feel those. Many people used this method in bringing amazing changes in their lives.

Let us see the steps to be followed to achieve self-hypnosis:

1] The very first thing, you have to decide what you want to accomplish with self-hypnosis. For example, you may plan to give yourself auto-suggestions to increase your self-confidence. Try to make your affirmations in present tense such as, "I am enthusiastic and confident."

2] It is better to write down the affirmations before practicing self-hypnosis. It becomes easier to visualize the affirmations already written. Listening and visualizing those assertions puts more energy in the process.

3] Choose a calm and quiet place to practice self-hypnosis. It is always better to practice at the same place and time at primitive stage. Once you master self-hypnosis, all these things become unimportant.

4] Sit in a comfortable chair. You may prefer a chair with high back, so that you can lean back comfortably. Sitting is preferable to lying down unless your goal is to fall asleep.

5] Breath deeply with gently closed eyes. Instruct yourself to relax completely. You can do this by tightening your muscles, hold for about three seconds, and then loosen completely. Relax each organ of your body, from scalp to toe, instructing it one by one.

6] Now imagine yourself going down the staircase. Count steps slowly, one by one, while going down. Ten…Nine…. Eight…etc.

7] Imagine that as you come down to the floor after counting one, there is a feather bed lying on the floor. Soft and comfortable. You can lie on it calmly. Feel the comfortable, joyous state and then slowly start your instructions which you wrote down in the beginning.

8] Continue to breathe deeply and evenly as you repeat your affirmations. You can also say those loudly if you wish.

9] When you are satisfied and complete your suggestions, get ready slowly to come up the stairs. Count slowly, One.. Two… Three… etc. as you are climbing up the stairs this time. You can instruct to open your eyes at Ten.

10] After reaching Ten, you can open your eyes slowly as per the instructions. You start controlling your mind and your consistent powerful affirmations make a positive effect on your subconscious mind during this process.

You have to close your eyes and relax your body completely. Imagine waves of relaxation running down your body from your scalp to toes, washing out all stress. Let the waves run with your breathing. Feel the muscles of your body relaxing as the waves of relaxation wash over those.

To deepen this state you can use suggestions. This can be as simple as saying something to yourself, "I am feeling relaxed and comfortable. With every breath I am becoming more and more relaxed… "Then mix your own prepared affirmations with these.

You also can record your affirmations (including relaxation) and just listen to it quietly by lying down with closed eyes. Some people find it more comfortable.

The hypnotic state can be categorized into three parts. Light, Medium and Deep hypnotic state. There are some tests to ascertain the depth of your hypnotic state. It implies how far you have progressed. As you deepen the hypnotic state, you can accomplish the progressive tests. Let us see the tests now:

Test 1

If you are able to close your eyelids at a specific count (decided by you), it is the first test to determine whether you have gone under hypnotic state or not.

Test 2

This is called the 'swallowing' test. You have to give suggestions to yourself that during the count of ten, you will get an irresistible urge to swallow one time. You may further suggest that this will happen even before you reach the count of ten. You then begin the count,' One… my throat is parched…and I feel an irresistible urge to swallow one time…Two.. my lips are becoming very dry …. Three ……. My throat feels very dry………. Four … before I reach the count of ten the urge to swallow one time becomes irresistible because my lips and throat are so dry………Five…………. Once I swallow I shall no longer have the urge to swallow again, and as I swallow one time, I shall fall to a deeper and sounder state of hypnosis…………….'

Continue with these suggestions by affirming and repeating the suggestions about swallowing. Once you actually swallow, you discontinue the suggestion and instead give yourself suggestions that you are falling into an increasingly deeper, sound, hypnotic state and whatever constructive suggestions you now give yourself will work for you. Then you practice visual imagery, seeing yourself the way you want to be while fortifying this image with forceful and positive suggestions. You can close by giving yourself suggestions that you will enter the hypnotic state whenever you relax for five minutes and count decided numbers.

For each progressive test, it is usually necessary to have accomplished the preceding tests. Once these two tests are accomplished, you can go for the next test to determine the depth of your hypnotic state.

Test 3

This is known as the 'hand tingling' test. You have already accomplished test 1 and 2 and you are in a completely relaxed state. Now give yourself the following suggestion, "As I count to ten and even before I reach the count ten, I shall feel a light tingling or numb feeling in my right hand." As you slowly begin the count of ten, you keep repeating suggestions to the effect that your right hand is beginning to tingle. You can imagine while taking suggestions how you feel when your hand actually becomes numb. As you practice this procedure, it will work with great effect. The most important point to be remembered is to ensure that you give yourself a posthypnotic suggestion and the tingling or numb sensation will disappear as you count a decided number.

The key to achieving a greater depth of hypnosis lies in visualizing yourself going deeper with each attempt and accomplishing progressive hypnotic tests. You have to use each step to enhance a greater receptivity for the next progressive test. As you couple this approach with posthypnotic suggestions that you will go deeper and deeper into the hypnotic state at a given stimulus, you set into motion a conditioned response mechanism which must ultimately guide you into a profound state of hypnosis.

Test 4

This is called the 'foot' test. This can be accomplished while sitting or lying down. The idea of this test is to imagine that your feet are stuck to the floor or that your legs are so heavy that they are impossible to raise until you reach a certain count. It is best to begin this test by trying to capture a heavy feeling in your legs. You give yourself specific suggestions such as, "As I count to five, I shall notice a very heavy, relaxed and pleasant feeling in both legs. It is a very comfortable feeling, a feeling of complete relaxation." You then begin the count of ten; following out the idea of the other previous tests you have successfully accomplished. Once you get a heavy, relaxed feeling you use the visual imagery technique to try to picture your legs stuck to the floor. After that, you can suggest, "As I continue to count to ten, I shall find that it will be impossible for me to raise my legs. I shall try at the count of ten but it will be absolutely impossible to raise my legs until I count to fifteen. At that time, I shall be able to raise my legs easily and the heavy feeling will leave as well."

You then continue with the count giving yourself appropriate suggestions. At the count of fifteen, you actually try to raise your legs. Let us assume at this point that you have finally succeeded in getting the foot test to work correctly and you are now ready for test number five.

Test 5

This is called the 'hand levitation' test. In this test, the goal is to get your hand to slowly rise and touch your chin. Once it touches your chin, you enter into a still, deeper state and lower your hand slowly to your side. This test is actually combined with the hand tingling test number 3. Since you have been successful with test number three, the rest is rather simple. This time as you work test number 3, aim for a light, pleasant feeling in your right hand. Once you get this reaction, you give yourself suggestions that your right hand now rise and touch your chin. As soon as it does, you will fall into deeper state and lower your hand. You can use the suggestions, "As I count to ten and even before I reach ten, I shall have an irresistible impulse to slowly raise my hand to my chin. As I progress with the counting, my hand will slowly rise and the impulse will become stronger and stronger. As soon as my hand touches my chin, the impulse will leave. I will then keep my hand aside and fall into deep, hypnotic state." Then you start giving posthypnotic suggestions to yourself.

You need not attempt to memorize the exact phraseology for any of the tests. The timing of the suggestions is the paramount consideration in attaining successful results.

One thing we must remember, whether we call it, Autosuggestion, Positive thinking, Meditation, Yoga, Affirmations or Self Hypnosis we are in reality talking about similar things. All these require certain basic prerequisites to work effectively for you. Keep in mind that the suggestions are being filtered into the subconscious mind which does not question, doubt, analyze or dispute the efficacy of all these suggestions. We have to be very careful while preparing the suggestions. At basic stage it is always advisable to use affirmations discussed by a consulting hypnotist.

Many people expect immediate results when they begin to use self-hypnosis. If they don't get the results they anticipated immediately they want to know, "What is wrong?" In reality, nothing is wrong. They need to do some more practicing. It takes some time to acquire proficiency.

Self-hypnosis finally works because you are constantly conditioning your subconscious to react in a positive, constructive manner. The program must, of necessity, become automatic in nature. When it does, you will suddenly find yourself feeling the way you wanted to and doing things that you set out to do with the aid of self-hypnosis. You actually cultivate those feelings that you want.

The suggestions are just as effective whether given aloud or mentally. You have to develop confidence while giving yourself suggestions. Giving effective suggestions cannot proceed in a hesitant manner. Those must be given in enthusiasm and anticipation. If you follow these instructions, you will derive the benefits you seek in the shortest possible time and witness the positive, tangible results of your suggestions and efforts.

Affirmations are always used as a part of self-hypnosis. Affirmations are positive statements (based on rational thinking) made by ourselves to counter stress and unpleasant thoughts.

Here is a sample self-hypnosis script I use during my hypnosis spiral but which you can adapt and modify.

'Now as I relax, my gaze is getting more and more concentrated. My eyes are becoming very heavy and tired. It is difficult to keep my eyelids open. Now as I count slowly from one to ten. One… my eyelids are getting closed slowly. Two… it is difficult to keep my eyes open now. Three…… my eyelids are gently and completely closed now. Four…feel relaxed and comfortable with closed eyes. Five……. Six…… feeling calm and quite. Seven………. Eight…… completely relaxed.

Nine…………enjoying a unique happiness. Ten……… slowly I am dropping down in drowsy state…..

I am sinking down into a drowsy state where everything is calm and quiet. I can just feel the deeply, relaxed state …. I am floating in a fluffy cloud …. Each organ of my body is completely relaxed…. My mind is free of all concerns and worries……. My nerves are calm and free of all tensions…. My entire body and mind are in perfect harmony……. Nothing from the outside can disturb my harmonious relaxed state………

I am in deep… and peaceful sleep………. My subconscious is accepting all my affirmations happily……………. My willpower is increasing immensely…………….I can concentrate more and more on any task…the power of my memory is enhanced tremendously............ ....I am entirely free of all types of fear, anxiety and tensions...................I will remain free of any kind of addiction............Power of my subconscious mind is increased a lot...........All these affirmations are very powerful and easily accepted by my subconscious mind for my benefit on permanent basis......... It will help me lifelong.......... Every day in every way I am becoming more and more successful......................'

If you are doing this practice at bedtime, then you can directly continue the affirmations till you asleep. If you want to do it within a stipulated time, you need to take post-hypnotic suggestions to come out of this state.

You can add visualization for better results for some specific outcome. You can use various symbols or a person in visualization to put more weight to understand and execute easily by your subconscious mind. Achieving hypnosis is a matter of directing a suggestibility that we already possess in the channels.

Let us see how to take post-hypnotic suggestions:

You can give yourself a specific count while instructing to awake or you can simply give plain instructions to awake from a self-hypnotic state. These are called post-hypnotic suggestions.

You can say, "I shall now open my eyes and wake up feeling fine," or you also use, "As I count one to five, I will open my eyes and wake up feeling wonderfully well and refreshed…. One…feeling good……. Two……becoming alert slowly ……. Three…………Four……….and Five………I am fully awake, my eyes are open and feeling energetic and cheerful!

The results of hypnosis are overwhelmingly positive and effective. It is a method of communication with your subconscious mind which induces a trance state for better results.

14 GROWING AS AN ENTREPRENEUR

I added this chapter since it covers all aspects of this book so far from discovery to hypnotic success habits, goal-setting and determination. Being an entrepreneur is something that a lot of people dream of becoming. It's a great dream to have and there are so many avenues open to the person who's willing to put in the effort to make the business succeed. This chapter is an overview of what you can achieve online when you have the following:

- Passion
- Motivation
- Determination
- Self-discovery
- Goals and Success habits
- The desire for freedom

I also want to sew the seed and wet the whistle for your ongoing journey in life and amazing potential success. I am going to be talking about how anyone, yes YOU can be successful online just by leveraging a bit of your time and motivation. You can make money residually and enjoy more time doing the things you like to do with it.

When you focus on something, it means that you're paying attention. But with the way we praise multi-tasking today, we've learned to give things our *divided* attention. When you create all these ideas and concepts sometimes as an entrepreneur driven to success, it is easy to get carried away.

So being divided and not focused is bad in relationships and bad in business. What happens when we get too many irons in the fire is that we become scattered. We're trying to do too many different things at once and we end up not doing any of them well.

There is a fine balance. You don't want to become so focused on one task that you overlook other ways to make money. There's a way that you can streamline your business so that you're able to do what you choose and do it well.

When you become an entrepreneur, you have a strong desire to succeed. If the desire to succeed was all that was needed, then the world be filled with nothing but success stories.

But desire alone won't keep you from failing and you may have experienced countless failures on your entrepreneurial journey. What you need to do is to take a step back and look at what you've been doing that *hasn't* worked for you. I know many of you can relate to that by counting your clients or show bookings.

Once you can identify what's not working and what you're struggling with, you can then find success by making changes. You need to understand what's gone wrong despite your best efforts.

Fear of Failure

Did you know that it's not failure that keeps people from trying? The world is full of examples of people who failed multiple times and yet ultimately found success. There's something worse than failing - and that's fear of failure because often, fear of failure keeps you from even trying anything at all.

There are some solid reasons behind having a fear of failure. No one disputes that. You might be hesitant to put yourself out there because you're afraid that people are going to laugh at you or your business idea.

Remember that people laughed at Henry Ford, too - and yet he became a well-known success story. You might be concerned that you'll end up failing and be humiliated. There are countless numbers of online success stories.

There are gurus in our industry who share their failures with their mailing list and talk about it on their website. They do this because failure was part of the journey, it wasn't the *end* of the journey.

You can overcome a fear of failure by learning to recognize it for what it is. Failure is never the end unless you give up.

It's a stepping stone that many people have walked on to reach the success that they dream of having.

Sometimes a fear of failure comes because we're afraid to make mistakes. But making mistakes is how you reach your goals - simply because you're not perfect. There's yet to be a single fail-proof human being on the Earth.

Instead of fearing failure, embrace it. Use it as something that you can learn from. Cut off the negative sound bytes in your mind. This is what plays in your head telling you that you're right to be afraid of failure, that you're not good enough, that you're not smart enough, that you're not talented enough, or not educated enough.

It's this sound byte that has a loop so that it will play on forever as long as you allow it. Negative thoughts of what you can't accomplish become a reality. Kick the glass-is-empty mindset to the curb and replace it with one that's optimistic.

The thought of pouring your heart into something and not making it a reality? Fear has been identified as False Evidence Appearing Real (That one was for Wayne Lee) We often have a habit of creating worst case scenarios in our minds that never come to fruition. Let go of the fear of failure and go after what you want.

Frustration with Technical Tasks

It's easy to get frustrated when you come across a technical task that you don't know how to do. When you're ready to move forward and get stuck by a lack of know-how, it can start that negative chatter running through your head again.

But keep in mind that no one has all of the knowledge they need to do everything. None of us are born knowing what we need to do. We learn as we grow and the same holds true when it comes to being a successful Hypnotist for example.

You might not know how to set up a blog and if you've never done it before, it's understandable that you wouldn't know how to get started. But in today's age, the Internet gives us a world of knowledge right at our fingertips.

If you don't know how to set up a blog, you can pull up a video on how to do it and then follow the instructions step by step until you're finished. Some people already know how to build a blog, but they don't know how to set up call-to-action buttons or how to add a shopping cart.

All of this type of information can easily be found in video tutorials. You can take the time to go through the video and pause it at each step as you implement the task. And there are hundreds of videos out there that address every technical task question you might have.

You can also join forums and post a question when you need help with a specific task. Many of these forums are filled with people who have already traveled the path that you're now on. These people freely share the knowledge that they have with others.

If you're trying to work with software and can't quite grasp it, you can also look this up with videos. You can also go to a search engine, type in the name of the software and add the word manual after it.

There are often PDF manuals for software available that will walk you through whatever it is that you need to do. You'll learn as you go along. Months down the road, you'll be amazed at what you've learned and then you'll be in a position to help someone else when they have a question about a task.

But keep in mind that there will always be a technical task that you might not know how to do because learning should never stop when you're an entrepreneur. You want your business to succeed and that means growth.

Any time there's growth with a business, there will be new things you have to handle. Give technical tasks a shot and if you get stuck, you can also go on a marketing forum and simply ask a very specific question telling people where you got stuck so that they can help.

Complacency Issues

You've heard the story about how if you put a frog in a pot of boiling water, he'll jump right out. But if you put a frog in water and slowly turn up the heat, he'll boil to death. While this is a myth, it's also a metaphor for life and shines the light on how you need to take charge to prevent complacency from setting in.

Complacency means that you are content with where you're at in life and with what you're doing. You've found your comfort zone and you're sticking with it. Being complacent is not a good thing because what it does is keep you stuck exactly where you are.

When you are complacent, you don't try to learn and improve your skills or your business. You don't aim for growth and you don't try new things that can help your success. What happens then is that it can become easy to lose your purpose for your business.

It can also be easy for lack of inner leadership to develop and things just fall by the wayside. The problem that arises most often when people reach a level of complacency is that they don't want to make an effort to do anything to change their lot in life, but they want to bring in more money.

Complacency and the desire to make more money aren't compatible. If you want more money, you don't get to be satisfied with the status quo. Since money isn't going to rush toward you when you're complacent, you have to do something about it.

You have to be proactive. You have to do something to change your mindset so you develop a hunger for success. What this means is that you have to gain more knowledge.

When you've reached a certain skill-set, nothing is ever going to change if you don't level up. You have to learn new things and you need to do it consistently to keep on growing and earning money.

That means that you're going to have to put more effort into your business. Some people think that once they've reached a certain level in business, it will always stay that way.

They think they'll always make money and that the money will just grow without them having to do anything to make that happen. That's not true. Money is brought in based on your efforts, so it's time to adopt new habits of learning and trying new ideas.

In today's world, when you start a business, it can be easy to become overloaded with excitement. It often happens because there are countless options available. One of the things that entrepreneurs have to be on guard against is shiny new object syndrome.

This is what happens when there are so many ideas that you want to try them, all so you hop from one idea to the next. It always feels like the newest idea is going to be great.

We find a new technique, new software, new tools and we chase after them. The beginning of something is always exciting because it holds the promise of success. It's what we've always been waiting for - this new idea or tool - so we have to do it or have it.

The problem with so many options is that it can cause you take off down various paths and end up preventing you from actually accomplishing anything at all. It's a lack of attention and focus that can derail your business if you're not careful.

Because when you're chasing the newest idea, you're not spending time on your business. You're not focusing on the things that matter with it. When you experience shiny new object syndrome, it can make you a jack of all trades and a master of none.

You are so busy chasing whatever is new and comes along that you don't complete the tasks that you should do in order to make your business successful. So what happens is you lose time and money on things that are wrong for your business.

You can get caught up in information overload, too - just like you can with shiny new object syndrome. When you have information overload, there's too much data for you to take it all in.

It's hard to know what to process and how to make a choice when there's too much information. If you have shiny new object syndrome, you might be able to start a hundred projects, but you won't follow through with any of them.

You'll end up getting about halfway done and then something new will come along and off you go again. With information overload, you can end up feeling paralyzed and unsure of what decisions to make, so in the end, you don't make a decision at all.

You can stop both of these from happening. With shiny new object syndrome, when something new comes along, always ask yourself if you have something that needs to be finished.

If there's something waiting for you to work on, don't get involved in another project until the other one is complete. With information overload, only take in the information you need to complete your task. Focus on one portion of information at a time. Remember that it's better to do one thing well than to do a dozen things poorly.

Do You Feel Like You're Always Working Yet Going Nowhere?

This feeling is a symptom. It's your internal radar trying to let you know that you're too scattered. You're all over the place with your business and it's not going to get any better if you don't make some changes.

Something that can cause you to feel like you're always working and getting nowhere is having too many niches. You're involved in so many different ideas that you can't give your full attention to any of them.

There's just not enough time, not enough money and not enough of you to go around for all of the niches that you want to be part of. Instead of being part of fifteen different niches that are struggling and stressing you out and causing you to work hard with little in return, cut back to a couple of niches that you can devote yourself to and watch them take off.

Obviously, you need a strategy in business. You have to have a workable plan in order to bring in a steady income. But a problem (or multiple problems) can arise when you have too many strategies.

You might be an entrepreneur who wants to be involved with affiliate marketing. This isn't a bad thing and it can turn into a steady income stream. But this is an area of marketing that takes time to build and you have to put some effort into it.

If you could devote yourself solely to affiliate marketing, you could make a decent amount of money with it. What happens is people add to it. They turn around and add info product creations.

Maybe that's you. You've seen people earn money with their own product creations and you decide that you want a piece of that pie. So you create a product and you put it out there.

So now, you have both the affiliate marketing and the product creation to keep up with. You feel like this may not be enough, and you might as well add coaching to the mix.

So you throw that in. You offer your advice to other people so that you can teach them to do what you've done. Now with three streams of income, things are getting a little hectic.

You might reach the point where you're forced to choose between putting out the latest product creation update or investing the time you do have in the coaching side of your business.

And don't forget - there's the affiliate marketing, too. You start to feel some pressure when you realize that you could make even more money if you offer services.

Someone comes along and they don't know how to create a product from start to finish and launch it, so you'll do that for them and they can just pay you. Or, what about a joint venture?

You could get involved in that. Before you know it, you have several opportunities and they're all good ones, but now - because you're so busy giving a little of yourself to each area, stretching yourself thin - none of them are the success that you'd hoped they'd become.

Each area of your business needs your full attention and planning. They have to be nurtured. Handling business endeavors using a drive-by method doesn't work well.

Are You Stuck in One Online Business That's Holding You Back?

There's no doubt that you can make money with an online business. Unfortunately, too many entrepreneurs lose sight of the fact that building any business takes some time to get off the ground.

If you decide that you want to become an affiliate marketer, you can make a steady income that could be pretty good. But it's not going to happen quickly.

Depending on which business you promote products for, it can take a while to get paid from these companies. That's because the people for whom you do the promotion get their money from the manufacturer or seller first.

Then they settle everything 60-90 days later. So if you expected that you would hang your affiliate marketing shingle one week and then get paid the next, you'll be disappointed.

Not only does it take time to get paid for the promotions, but it's going to take you time to build traffic to your site. You won't get any traction right out of the gate.

You have to build it - and that's where patience and motivation will keep you going even when you don't see results. You don't want to put all of your hopes and dreams of making money into one online business - especially if you start with affiliate marketing.

Instead, what you can do to bring in money faster is you can promote info products. When you do this, you get a return on your efforts faster because the hold back time to settle payment isn't as long of a wait – in fact, in many cases, it's instant.

The good news is that you don't even have to step outside your chosen niche to make this additional income. If you're in the weight loss niche, you can choose to promote weight loss info products or health products.

It can be things for whatever niche you're already involved in. Maybe you're someone who is already doing an info product and you want to bring in more money.

In that case, what you can do is to look to do promotions for people or brands who already have the traction to move the product. Make sure the offers complement the ones you're developing so that your audience always sees the relevancy in your promotion.

Learn the Art of Following Through

Some people will start a business project, get it partially done and walk away. This sometimes happens because they might feel as if they lack the knowledge of how to finish it.

Other times, people will start a project and then quit it because something new catches their attention that seems more enticing. Whatever the reason, if you're not careful, you can end up with dozens of half started business projects.

It's important that you follow through with what you start because unfinished tasks can weigh on your subconscious mind. You first need to be able to clearly identify what it is that you're hoping to accomplish with the project you've chosen to spend your time and energy on.

This definition gives you a goal to work toward and it helps you keep your motivation level high so that you can push forward when you want to give up. Know up front what it's going to take to complete the project.

If you know ahead of time that it's going to take long hours and you won't see fast results, this will help you keep going. You might not be able to see the results quickly, but in your mind you'll have that mental image of what it will be.

This allows you to maintain focus. Make sure that your strategy for follow through includes having the right tools and the right knowledge to get the job done. Buy what you have to have to complete the task and bring in outside help if you have to.

For example, if you can create the info product, but you can't do the graphics, you either have to learn how to do it yourself or you have to hire someone to do it for you.

If taking the time to learn it yourself will keep you from following through because you already have so much going on that you can't take the time to study anything new, then you're better off paying someone else.

Being an entrepreneur often means that you don't have someone waiting in the wings to tell you when you have to get a project done. You have to learn the art of following through by assigning due dates to each step of the project.

This helps give you accountability and keeps you on track so that you do finish. With follow through, you have to learn to recognize when enough is enough. You don't want to overdo a project.

Some people will constantly tweak a project. They keep finding one more thing they want to change or fix. When that happens, the project doesn't get finished because you don't ever let it go.

Ask yourself two questions to help you figure out if the job is complete or not. Did you do it to the best of your abilities? Did you accomplish what you set out to do? If you can say *yes* to both of those, then it's completed and you need to move on.

How to Have Multiple Business Branches the Right Way

There's nothing wrong with having several different branches in your business. But branches have to be added on, you can't simply try to grow them all at once, or the foundation of your business won't be able to sustain them.

The right way to have multiple branches is by building them slowly. You always want to start out with the one that's going to be the money maker. You need this one so that you can live on the income and take care of your bills while you build up the other branches.

So choose the branch that brings in the money first. What this will mean for most people is something like service providing. When you provide a service to someone else, they pay you faster than if you're trying to create something.

If you provide services for someone else, that also gives you the money to invest back in your own business. This helps keep your business growing. After you have a steady stream of income that can sustain you, that's when you can have the financial flexibility to start adding on to your business.

But don't add more than one thing at a time. You can start by doing something like creating an info product. You can work on this while you're providing a service to someone else in the meantime.

Work on your first info product and get it available to the public. That will start to sell, but while interest is growing in that product, you should be busy creating another info product.

In the beginning, you might have to do all of the work involved with the product creation yourself. However, as this branch of your business grows stronger, you can start to outsource some of the work.

You keep creating info products and adding them to your branch until this area is doing well for you financially. When it's steady and thriving, then you move on to another branch, such as coaching or ad revenue.

Work that branch until it's succeeds as well. By taking the time to focus on a single branch at a time, you avoid spreading yourself too thin. You're able to concentrate and nurture each branch toward success.

Set Up a Business That You Have Time For

When you want to be an entrepreneur, you have to know the value of time management. Without it, your business might not make it. If you ask some people what time management is, they'll answer that it means managing your time wisely.

While that's part of, that's a small part. Time management is more than knowing when to do something and scheduling a slot for it in your day. It's knowing that the task you're planning to do is an investment.

You're putting hours into something and hoping to get a return on that effort. When you set up a business that you have time for, you can have the kind of returns that you're looking to receive.

Don't plan to cram your day full of to-do tasks associated with your business. That's not time management. Time management for an entrepreneur means that you block out enough time for each project so that it has the best opportunity to be a success.

You have to have the time set aside to make sure that project takes off and thrives once you're done. You don't gain in business by rushing through your projects.

If you have so much going on that you can't afford to allocate enough time to each project, then you have to scale back. It's better to let stuff go and have one or two projects be successful than it is to have a dozen mediocre projects or failures.

When you give a project the dedicated hours that it needs, you actually improve your time management through effectiveness rather than lose time. You'll discover that you're more efficient the more time you're able to give a project.

It's far better for you to spend 4 hours of your day working to create value for one of your business branches than it is to rush through half an hour on multiple projects or spend half an hour trying to get through some tasks for each task.

It's harder to focus like that and harder to give 100% of your effort. Plus, if you do that, you'll end up scatterbrained and feeling as if you're not really accomplishing anything anyway.

Remember that with all businesses, there will come a time for pruning in order for new growth to take place. You want to make sure you're doing all that you can to allow for your business to be able to thrive.

If at any time, you realize that you need to cut back, consider whether or not it will be a temporary move, setting something on the back burner, or if you're going to get rid of it for good. Sometimes it can ease your mind to lighten your load.

For more business and entrepreneurial advice obtain my book "Selling Hypnotically" from my website or Amazon.

ABOUT THE AUTHOR

Richard Barker is a world-renowned professional hypnotist, comedy stage entertainer, media source, author and keynote speaker. He has spent the last 20 years entertaining audiences all over the world with his dazzling hypnosis show in 38 countries. As the Incredible Hypnotist, Richard brings his charm and experience to blow the minds of audiences, media professionals, celebrities and corporate clients. Offstage, Richard has improved the lives of countless clients that needed hypnosis to get over an obstacle, phobia or behavior. Using his Master's Degree in Education, he is constantly helping others understand the true power of hypnosis.

The Incredible Hypnotist has been featured in countless media outlets and publications. Richard's work can see been on: The Today Show, The Late Late Show with James Corden, ET Entertainment Tonight, Reader's Digest, Huffington Post, Glamour Magazine, Sports Illustrated, Marie Claire, US Weekly, Google Talks, Health Magazine, Self Magazine, Men's Fitness, InStyle, YouTube Creator Summit, CBS, NBC, FOX, ABC, CMT as well as many major news shows and publications across the globe.

Richard chooses to focus most of his efforts on comedy hypnosis performances because he feels it's a marvelous introduction into the world of hypnosis. "I give the people a compelling, fascinating and entertaining entry into hypnosis and after that, they become curious as to what the mind can actually do." Although he is a comedy stage hypnotist,

Richard Barker constantly re-frames the entertainment aspect of hypnosis back to the hypothetical question, "What if hypnosis could help you with a health-related issue?"